PENGUIN PARALLEL TEXTS

ITALIAN SHORT STORIES I

I0971837

ITALIAN SHORT STORIES I

RACCONTI ITALIANI

———

Edited by Raleigh Trevelyan

PENGUIN BOOKS

PENGUIN BOOKS

Published by the Penguin Group
Penguin Books Ltd, 80 Strand, London WC2R 0RL, England
Penguin Putnam Inc., 375 Hudson Street, New York, New York 10014, USA
Penguin Books Australia Ltd, 250 Camberwell Road, Camberwell, Victoria 3124, Australia
Penguin Books Canada Ltd, 10 Alcorn Avenue, Toronto, Ontario, Canada M4V 3B2
Penguin Books India (P) Ltd, 11 Community Centre, Panchsheel Park, New Delhi – 110 017, India
Penguin Books (NZ) Ltd, Cnr Rosedale and Airborne Roads, Albany, Auckland, New Zealand
Penguin Books (South Africa) (Pty) Ltd, 24 Sturdee Avenue, Rosebank 2196, South Africa

Penguin Books Ltd, Registered Offices: 80 Strand, London WC2R 0RL, England

www.penguin.com

First published 1965
37

Printed in England by Clays Ltd, St Ives plc
Set in Monotype Baskerville

ISBN-13: 978–0–140–02196–7
ISBN-10: 0–140–02196–5

www.greenpenguin.co.uk

Penguin Books is committed to a sustainable future
for our business, our readers and our planet.
The book in your hands is made from paper
certified by the Forest Stewardship Council.

CONTENTS

INTRODUCTION

Primarily this book is for those learning Italian. It is also intended to be representative of short-story writing by major Italian authors since the war. Thus the translators have had two tasks: they have had to keep as close as possible to the original texts, and at the same time they have tried to capture enough of the spirit and character of their authors to make the stories readable and enjoyable to the layman who may know nothing of the language but is simply interested in modern Italian literature.

At the end of the book students will find notes on uncommon words or phrases, colloquialisms, allusions, and difficult constructions. These notes are intended to fill in the gaps left by common sense and a medium-sized dictionary. For it has been assumed that students have some grounding in Italian. Figures referring to the notes are printed in the Italian texts only, so that the English versions can be read without interruption. The stories have been printed in chronological order of original publication in Italy, but the student may find it easier to start with Moravia, follow on with Ginzburg and Cassola, and end with Gadda.

There are, of course, other important Italian short-story writers besides those that have been chosen, but most have had to be ruled out for various reasons. Either their stories are too long, as in the case of Bassani or Pasolini, who also often uses Roman dialect. Or else, like Vittorini, they have not written short stories since the war. Since the book is limited to eight authors, personal preferences play their part too. Manzini, Morante, and Ortese have had to be sacrificed to Ginzburg. Alvaro, Arpino, Romano, Rosso, and Sciascia have also had to be put to one side. Others certainly eligible were Bigiaretti, Bilenchi, Buzzati,

Cicognani, Comisso, Landolfi, and Tobino. Jovine, who died in 1950 and has many admirers, might well be considered an omission.

Again, the aim has been to find stories of which English translations have not hitherto appeared in book form. Fortunately it has been possible, as in the case of Pratolini, to include specimens of some of the authors' best known work. Pavese's story was written in 1943, but first published in 1945. Otherwise all the others are post-war. Some have been deliberately selected as illuminating earlier, significant phases of a writer's career, when it would have been as easy to find a more recent example. The range of the stories has been kept wide. There is a ghost story. There are pictures of poverty at its lowest ebb and over-sophistication at its most languid. There are stories with overtones of social conflict, portraits of childhood, adolescence, and gropings towards maturity. Some stories are pessimistic; others are the opposite, and one is frankly exuberant. Three stories, in fact, have children as main characters – a genre in which Italian writers can excel.

Although at least half the authors selected for this book had already made a literary mark for themselves before 1940, it is fair to say that all of them have been affected very deeply by the catalyst of the war – by the release from Fascism and the fight for political independence that this involved. They are all, even Gadda (whose work in any case is full of sarcastic references to Fascist times), a part of that extraordinary renaissance in the arts that has burst out in Italy since the war ended. It is worth noting, for instance, that Calvino and Cassola drew effectively on their experiences with the partisans in their earliest work. Pavese, Moravia, and Ginzburg suffered persecution.

These authors, therefore, are representative of the literary generation that developed as a consequence of the war years. New writers, who never shared their experiences, are emerging. Yet none can escape what happened twenty years ago. Parallel with the post-war artistic revival there

has been the equally remarkable economic boom. This too cannot help having its consequences on the writer. There has been a shift in the whole economic structure; private incomes, to some extent, have been levelled out, even though there are still social discrepancies in Italy as marked as nearly anywhere in Europe. Culture, with a capital C, has become an industry, and this has partly accounted for the dramatic growth in the reading public. The very successful film business, with its glittering publicity and personality cults, has had its importance. Of the authors included here Soldati is the one who in this respect has perhaps been the most involved, though most have felt the effect of the cinema in some way or other.

Pratolini's story is among his most admired, and is thus typical. With a boy as its first-person narrator and full of references to his beloved Florence, it is like a small sharp detail in a crowded canvas. Again, *Pavese*'s story displays typical themes: the contrast between maturity and inexperience, the yearning for comradeship and the fear of being alone, the way marriage can break old ties yet create a new, inner privacy. *Cassola*, in his early period, wrote about groups of working-class men. His story, belonging to that period and written before the novels, deals partly with the wives of these men. His central character, although a hypocrite and a snob, is in contrast both physically and mentally a 'normal' person. *Calvino* here is shown at his most enchanting phase; there is no hint of any social or political problem. He shows a sheer joy in writing – for example, in the way he brings in the names, even dialect names, of the fish. *Gadda* the 'untranslatable' has been brilliantly served by Mrs Rawson. His story is an exception, in that it is without his customary, elaborate notes; on the other hand in this book it has been necessary to provide almost equally full explanations of his many typically ironic and literary allusions. As usual he is criticizing society, but he realizes well enough that by so doing he cannot change it. *Ginzburg*'s story is one of her most outstanding and very representative in content and

INTRODUCTION

style – bare and crisp, full of feminine detail, an overall sameness of tone. *Moravia*'s theme is one of his favourites: mental alienation, the fear of facing up to realities. 'The only person to whom you can tell everything, in this house, is myself,' says the provocative, indiscreet daughter at the end, and she is the last person who will be told. *Soldati*'s story is among his latest and his best. It has an almost Chekovian quality and is full of brooding atmosphere and nostalgia.

I have to thank the Casa Editrice Valentino Bompiani, Milan, for permission to include the story by Moravia; Giulio Einaudi Editore, Turin, for the stories by Calvino, Cassola, Ginzburg, and Pavese; Aldo Garzanti Editore, Milan, for the story by Gadda; Arnoldo Mondadori Editore, Milano, for those by Pratolini and Soldati. The translators have had a particularly difficult task and I am grateful to them for their patience and cooperation. I am very indebted to Dr Filippo Donini, Director of the Italian Institute in London, for his advice, and especially to Camillo Pennati, the poet, who has given up many hours of his time in helping me to select and edit this collection.

RALEIGH TREVELYAN

THE REMOVAL
VASCO PRATOLINI

Translated by Pamela Swinglehurst

LO SGOMBERO

La nonna ed io passammo da via de' Magazzini a via del Corno,[1] nell'autunno del '26. Eravamo rimasti noi due 'soli sulla faccia della terra', come lei diceva; e via de' Magazzini, al centro della città, aveva, con gli anni, conferito un nuovo valore alle sue case, gli appartamenti erano stati venduti uno ad uno. Un commerciante e sua moglie avevano acquistato quello in cui noi abitavamo: venivano da Torino e la casa gli serviva,[2] stavano in albergo nell'attesa; progettavano di cambiare piancito, di alzare un tramezzo per il bagno, fra ingresso e cucina; offersero una buonuscita[3] che la nonna rifiutò. Lo sfratto venne prorogato di tre mesi. Ora ci sentivamo assediati: i vecchi inquilini dello stabile ci avevano lasciato (e il sarto Masi, anarchico e ottantenne, aveva fatto in tempo a morirvi, conciliato con Dio, di crepacuore) cedendo il posto ai nuovi padroni delle mura: l'ingegnere del primo piano dirigeva di persona l'impianto della luce, del gas, i lavori di rimodernamento per il condominio.[4] Noi resistevamo, soli e isolati, col nostro lume a petrolio, il fornello a carbone, ricevendo sguardi di rimprovero, di ironia, minacce lungo le scale: impedivamo, rifiutandoci non so come, la costruzione di una moderna fossa biologica. E caparbia, in tanta apparente ingenuità, la nonna ripeteva loro:

«Mio marito fece stimare la casa, poi ci ripensarono e non ce la vollero piú vendere. Se ora si sono decisi, ecco le milleduecento lire della stima.»

«Trent'anni fa» le dicevano, «adesso costa ventimila, lei è stata interpellata per prima ed ha lasciato cadere l'offerta.»

THE REMOVAL

Grandmother and I moved from via de' Magazzini to via del Corno, in the autumn of '26. The two of us had been left 'alone on the face of the earth', as she used to say; and via de' Magazzini, in the centre of the city, had, with the passing of the years, bestowed a new value on its buildings, and one by one the apartments had been sold. A business man and his wife had bought the one in which we were living: they came from Turin and needed the house, for meanwhile they were living in a hotel; they were planning to renew the flooring, to put up a partition for the bathroom, between the entrance and the kitchen; they offered us compensation money which grandmother refused. The eviction order was suspended for three months. Now we felt ourselves besieged: the old tenants of the block had left us (and Masi the tailor, anarchist and octogenarian, had died there just in time, at peace with God, of a broken heart) making way for the new owners of the property: the engineer from the first floor was personally directing the installation of electric light and gas, and the modernization of the building. We continued to hold out, alone and isolated, with our oil lamp, our coal stove, receiving looks of reproof, of irony, threats all down the stairs: by somehow refusing it, we were hindering the construction of a modern cesspool. And grandmother, obstinate and with such apparent naïveté, used to repeat to them:

'My husband had the house valued, but then they had second thoughts and didn't want to sell it any more. If now they've made their minds up to it, here are the twelve hundred lire of the estimate.'

'Thirty years ago,' they told her, 'but now it costs twenty thousand. You were the first to be given the option and you let it go.'

«Non le ho forse pagate di pigione, ventimila lire, in questi trent'anni?»

«Perde la buonuscita, se si oppone allo sfratto. Con la buonuscita troverà da sistemarsi altrove, lei e suo nipote.»

«Stiamo bene dove stiamo» ella rispondeva. «Ci sono stata bene piú di trent'anni, e allevato figli e ... Del resto, non si trovano case per un fitto adeguato alla mia borsa. Con la buonuscita potrò pagarlo un anno, due, e poi? Mentre qui, piú di tanto non mi possono aumentare. Ho già dovuto vendere i mobili del salotto per trovarmi qualcosa da parte, all'occorrenza.»

«Vede, lo vede?» le dicevano. «Praticamente le basta una camera vuota con l'uso di cucina; e una camera, modesta, con l'uso di cucina, la buonuscita gliela garantisce per cinque anni almeno.»

«Ma in combutta con altri, senza piú libertà, e chissà dove, chissà in che strada, e con che gente. Ho abitato piú di trent'anni dove sono, mi ci sono nati e morti i figlioli, c'è morto mio marito . . .»

E sempre, come un intercalare ormai, e come un argomento tanto piú decisivo quanto piú puerile:

«È da trent'anni che sento Palazzo Vecchio⁵ battere le ore.»

Cosí resistevamo, col nostro lume a petrolio, lo scaldino e il campanello a tirante che non serviva piú. Avevano messo la placca coi bottoni elettrici alla porta di strada, verniciate le porte sulle scale, le targhe di ottone, le scale stesse imbiancate, sostituite le lastre del lucernario. E il nostro uscio, scortecciato allo zoccolo, il cartellino su cui avevo scritto a stampatello Casati, la griglia impolverata dal tempo erano una stonatura, un'offesa – fino alla mattina che mi accompagnai⁶ sfregando col carbone sul muro delle scale e l'ingegnere mi sorprese. Due giorni dopo, avvalendosi di una disposizione del Giudice che ne consentiva il diritto al

'Haven't I perhaps paid out twenty thousand lire in rent during these thirty years?'

'You'll lose the compensation money, if you resist the eviction order. With the compensation you'd find somewhere else to settle down, you and your grandson.'

'We're comfortable where we are,' she would answer. 'I've been at home here for over thirty years, and raised children and.... Anyway, there aren't any places to be found at a rent to suit my purse. With the compensation money I'd be able to pay for a year or two, and then? Whereas here there are limits to how much they can raise my rent. I've already had to sell the parlour furniture so as to have something put away, in case I need it.'

'There you are, you see?' they would say to her. 'In fact all you need is one empty room with use of kitchen. And your compensation money would guarantee you a room, a modest one, with use of kitchen, for at least five years.'

'But herded together with others, with no freedom any more, and who knows where, who knows in what street, and among what kind of people. I've been living where I am for more than thirty years, my children have been born and died here, my husband died here...'

And invariably, by now a kind of stock phrase, and as an argument as final as it was childish:

'For thirty years I've listened to the Palazzo Vecchio chiming the hours.'

In this way we went on resisting, with our oil lamp, the coke brazier and the doorbell you had to pull which no longer served any purpose. They had fixed the plate with the electric doorbells on the street door, the doors on the staircase had been varnished, the name plates were of polished brass, the stairs themselves freshly whitened, the glass panes of the skylight renewed. And our door, all scratched from wooden boots, the small card on which I'd printed Casati, the iron grille thick with the dust of years, these were an eyesore, an insult – until the morning when the engineer caught me scraping coal against the staircase wall. Two days later, taking advantage of a Court order

nuovo proprietario, ci entrarono in casa i muratori,
cominciarono dal salotto per aprirvi⁷ una vetrata. Dovemmo trasportare in camera il divano, il tavolo e le due
sedie che ancora lo arredavano. Ed erano ormai trascorsi
i secondi tre mesi, era un novembre di gelo, dietro le imposte serrate i rintocchi di Palazzo Vecchio avevano
un'eco lunga, sepolcrale, il silenzio della strada era
spaventoso quelle notti, e i sospiri della nonna simili a
una soffocata agonia: restavo desto ad ascoltarla, ragazzo, con l'allucinato timore che ella addormentatasi,
cessato il suo lamento, il sonno la consegnasse alla morte.

Poi fu il 24 novembre e arrivarono gli uscieri, ci
dettero altri sei giorni di tempo e siccome la nonna
si rifiutò ancora una volta di accettare l'intimazione di
sfratto, staccarono una delle puntine e attaccarono il
foglio sulla porta, sopra il cartellino. I muratori stavano
a guardare.

«Se mi permette»⁸ disse uno di loro, «credo che lei non
si renda conto della situazione.»

Era un uomo sui quarant'anni, dalla pronuncia vernacola, i baffi tagliati corti fino agli angoli della bocca,
portava il cappello lavorando.

«Si ritroverà col letto sulla strada, cosa spera?»

La nonna era poggiata di spalle alla finestra, volgeva
attorno lo sguardo, sulla parete abbattuta, sul piancito
rimosso, si teneva il labbro inferiore tra le gengive:

«Entrai in questa casa poco dopo sposata ... È perché sono una vecchia sola con un ragazzo.»

«È perché loro sono dalla parte della ragione» disse il
muratore. «Hanno o no comprato .»

«Anche mio marito voleva comprare ...»

«Sí» disse il muratore. «Quando uno piú uno faceva
due.»

E si offerse di aiutarci, sapeva di una camera vuota,

16

which granted the rights to the new owner, bricklayers invaded our home, and began in the parlour by making a glass door there. We had to shift into the bedroom the settee, the table, and the two chairs which still remained of the furniture. And by now the second three months had passed, and it was a freezing November. Behind the locked shutters the chimes of the Palazzo Vecchio had a long sepulchral echo, the silence of the streets was frightening those nights, and grandmother's sighs sounded like a smothered agony: I stayed awake listening to her, boy that I was, with the haunting fear that, when her moaning stopped, she might sink into the sleep that would hand her over to death.

Then it was the 24th November and the bailiffs arrived, and granted us a further six days' grace, and since grandmother refused once more to accept the eviction notice, they pulled out one of the drawing pins and stuck the paper on the door above the little card. The bricklayers stood around watching.

'If you'll forgive my saying so,' one of them offered, 'I don't think you altogether appreciate the situation.'

He was a man of about forty, with a local accent, his moustache cropped short at the corners of his mouth, and he wore a hat while he worked.

'You'll find yourself in the street with your bed, what else do you expect?'

Grandmother was leaning on her shoulder at the window, gazing round her at the demolished wall and the missing floorboards, biting her lower lip between her gums.

'I moved into this house soon after I was married. It's because I'm an old woman alone with a young boy.'

'It's because they're within their rights,' said the bricklayer. 'Have they bought the place or haven't they?'

'My husband also wanted to buy it . . .'

'Sure,' said the bricklayer. 'In the days when one and one made two.'

And he offered to help us, he knew of a vacant room,

'con uso di cucina', dove abitava un suo parente, in via del Corno, tra brave persone.

«A poco» disse. «Non sono venali.»

«Cosí fuori di mano» disse la nonna.

Il muratore sorrise:

«Vive qui da tanti anni e non sa dov'è via del Corno. Ma a due passi, si scende via de' Gondi⁹ e ci siamo.»

«Ah» esclamò la nonna, «ho capito, mi ci lasci pensare.»

A sera, e d'improvviso, rompendo il silenzio, da letto a letto, ella mi disse:

«Via del Corno non è una strada adatta a noi ...» Poi aggiunse: «Non bisogna lasciarli piú soli in casa, i muratori».

Ma non fu necessario: accertato che comunque ce ne saremmo dovuti andare entro la settimana, i lavori vennero sospesi. L'indomani volli vedere via del Corno, cosí prossima e anche a me sconosciuta: era un vicolo escluso al traffico e breve, ma popolato, rumoroso, assordante rispetto a via de' Magazzini, con puzzo di cavallo e biancheria appesa alle finestre. C'era un orinatoio sull'angolo, e mi sembrò che soltanto per questo vi si potesse sostare.

Finché, come il muratore aveva previsto, i nostri mobili si trovarono allineati sul marciapiede, e il piú giovane dei due uscieri, un biondo, ci chiese di ringraziarlo per averci fatto risparmiare le spese del facchino.

«Sembra uno stabile disabitato» commentò mentre insieme trasportavamo l'armadio. Rivolto alla nonna disse anche: «Non siamo noi, è la legge».

La nonna gli dette la mano. Ella aveva sperato in una nuova proroga, 'se non firmiamo, lo sfratto non diventerà mai esecutivo' mi diceva, intanto aveva dato la caparra in via del Corno. Ci saremmo dovuti adattare noi alla strada, 'giocoforza', dopo che cercando, in quei sei giorni, non ci s'erano offerte occasioni possibili o migliori.

'with use of kitchen', where one of his relations was living, in the via del Corno, among decent folk.

'It doesn't cost much,' he said. 'They're not grasping.'

'So out of the way,' said grandmother.

The bricklayer smiled.

'You've been living here for so many years and you don't know where via del Corno is. It's only a stone's throw from here, you just go down the via de' Gondi and you're there.'

'Ah,' grandmother exclaimed, 'I know, let me think it over.'

In the evening, quite out of the blue, breaking the silence as we lay in our beds, she said to me:

'Via del Corno isn't the kind of street for us. . . .' Then she added: 'We mustn't leave them alone in the house any more, those bricklayers.'

But it wasn't necessary: in the knowledge that we would anyway have to get out by the end of the week, work was suspended. The next day I wanted to have a look at the via del Corno, so near and unknown also to me: it was a short alley where traffic could not enter, but bustling, noisy, deafening compared with the via de' Magazzini, stinking of horses and with the washing hanging from the windows. There was a men's urinal on the corner, and it seemed to me that this could be the sole reason for halting there.

In the end, as the bricklayer had predicted, our bits of furniture found themselves lined up on the pavement, and the younger of the two bailiffs, a fair-haired man, asked us to thank him for saving us the expense of a porter.

'It feels like a deserted house' he remarked as we were all moving the cupboard. He turned to grandmother and added: 'It isn't our doing, it's the law.'

Grandmother shook hands with him. She had been hoping for a new delay, 'as long as we don't sign, they'll never put the eviction order into force' she would say to me, but meanwhile she had paid a deposit on the place in via del Corno. We were going to have to adapt ourselves to the street, willy-nilly, after searching throughout those six days, and no feasible or better bargains having presented themselves.

Ora io tornavo con un carretto preso a nolo, e i due uscieri ci aiutarono a caricarvi la nostra roba.

«Di piú non possiamo fare» disse il biondo, «siamo in ritardo» e ci lasciarono, noi soli adesso nel mezzo di via de' Magazzini, col barroccino carico di tutta la nostra roba, tanta da stare sul barroccino. La nonna teneva sotto il braccio l'"ingrandimento' della mamma, con la fotografia voltata sul suo petto. Sembrava serena, troppo per esserlo veramente, gli occhi asciutti, i gesti ordinati, come se giunto il momento la sua angoscia si compisse, nemmeno la sua voce tradiva un sentimento fuori dello ordinario. Tirava le corde che trattenevano le masserizie, per accertarsi che reggessero, che non mancasse nulla.

«C'è tutto» diceva. «I due lettini, la cassa della biancheria, il tavolo, l'armadio. Ce la facciamo con un solo viaggio. Ho fatto bene a vendere l'ottomana,[10] nella camera che abbiamo non ci sarebbe entrata. Le sedie le metteremo in cima quando ci muoviamo, il ritratto della mamma ce l'ho io, bene ... E ora?»

«Ora dobbiamo partire» dissi.

«Già»[11] ella continuò. «Le corde reggeranno, arriveremo in pochi minuti, i soldi li ho in tasca, la cassetta delle pentole sí, c'è ... Ma tu ce la farai?»

«Il carico è calibrato, è leggero.»

«È tutta la nostra casa» ella disse. «E andiamo a stare in una strada ... Ricordati, buongiorno buonasera e basta, è gente con la quale noi non abbiamo nulla da spartire, è la sventura che ci porta in mezzo a loro, ma per poco, un mese al massimo. Con un mese di tempo davanti a noi, troveremo di meglio, almeno in una strada com'è stata questa nostra per tanti anni, tra gente perbene.»

Erano le dieci di mattina, via de' Magazzini silenziosa e deserta, col suo spicchio di cielo tra le case, l'aria intirizziva le mani, i rari passanti ci rivolgevano

Now I was coming back with a hired handcart, and the two bailiffs helped us to load our stuff onto it.

'We can't do any more,' said the fair one, 'we're late,' and they left us, the two of us alone now in the middle of via de' Magazzini, with the barrow laden with all our belongings, just about as much as it would hold. Grandmother held under her arm the 'enlargement' of my mother, with the photograph facing her bosom. She was outwardly calm, too much to be really so, her eyes were dry, her movements unhurried, as if now that the moment had come her anguish was sated; not even her voice betrayed any unwonted emotion. She tugged at the cords which held the household effects, making sure they were securely tied and that nothing was missing.

'It's all here,' she said. 'The two small beds, the linen chest, the table, the cupboard. We can do it in one trip. I did well to sell the ottoman, we couldn't have got it into this room of ours. We'll put the chairs on top when we move off, I've got the picture of your mother, good. . . . And now?'

'Now we'd better get going,' I said.

'Yes yes, of course,' she went on. 'The ropes will hold, we'll be there in a few minutes, I've got the money in my pocket, there's the box of pans, there's. . . . But will you be able to manage?'

'It's evenly loaded, and not heavy.'

'It's our entire household,' she said. 'And now we're off to live in a street. . . . Remember now, good morning, good evening and no more, they're people with whom we have nothing in common, it's ill luck that takes us in their midst but it won't be for long, a month at the most. With a whole month ahead of us, we'll find something better, at least in a street such as this one of ours was for so many years, amongst decent folk.'

It was ten o'clock in the morning; the via de' Magazzini silent and deserted, with its sliver of sky between the houses, the air numbing our hands, the occasional passers-by turn-

uno sguardo e procedevano, un ciclista scampanellò a
ridosso[12] del nostro carico.

«Non son riuscita mai a capire» disse la nonna,
«perché di qui passa sempre poca gente, in centro come
siamo, con l'angolo su via Condotta che è un via vai.»

«Ma perché è una strada interna, bisogna passarci
apposta, non si accorcia il cammino, non ti pare? Un
po' come via del Corno. Lí c'è rumore perché ci sono gli
stallaggi e la gente è diversa, l'hai detto tu.»

«Già, non può essere educata come da noi, vive
sulla strada, fa cento mestieri, e di che genere. Dunque, c'è tutto.»

«Sí, c'è tutto» io dissi, «e non andiamo poi in capo al
mondo.»

«Già, già» ella ripeteva. Guardava su, le finestre,
parlava come al ritorno dopo una lunga assenza. «Sei
nato lí vedi? Quella aperta, a destra verso la doccia,
erano le undici di mattina, suppergiú quest'ora ...
Le abbiamo lasciate aperte tutte e due le nostre
finestre ... Tutte le altre sono chiuse, per forza» rispose a se stessa, «fa già freddo. Non mi ero accorta che
avessero messo le tendine.[13] È piú buio nelle stanze,
di questa stagione, con le tendine abbassate. La tua
mamma, non lo voleva capire. 'Le tiene forse il Masi?'
le dicevo, 'col lavoro che fa, d'inverno dovrebbe accendere il lume alle due ...'.»

«Ti devi decidere» le dissi.

Avevo impugnato le due stanghe e spinto avanti
il carretto, era leggero a portarsi, come mi aspettavo.
La nonna teneva il ritratto contro il petto, mi camminava di fianco, non si voltò piú, accelerò il passo
invece, fu a metà del carretto, appoggiò la mano a
tutelare il carico. Cosí uscimmo dalla nostra strada
incontro alla nuova, giú, discesa via de' Gondi, per-
correndo il breve tratto di piazza della Signoria, rasente
le case.

ing to glance at us and proceeding on their way, a cyclist ringing his bell as he passed our load.

'I have never been able to understand,' said grandmother, 'why there are always so few people passing here, right in the centre as we are, with the corner on via Condotta which is a constant bustle.'

'But because it's only a side street, you'd need to have a reason for coming along it, it isn't a short cut, don't you think that's why? Rather like via del Corno. It's noisy there on account of the stables and because the people are different, you've said so yourself.'

'Yes, yes, they can't be well bred like they are round here, they live in the street, they do a hundred different jobs, and what jobs. Well then, that's everything.'

'Yes, that's the lot,' I said, 'and anyway we aren't exactly going to the ends of the earth.'

'True true,' she kept repeating. She was looking up at the windows, talking as if she'd returned after a long absence. 'You were born there see? The open one, on the right near the drainpipe, it was at eleven in the morning, just about this time. . . . We've left both our windows open. . . . All the others are closed, of course,' she answered herself, 'it's cold already. I hadn't noticed that they'd put up the net curtains. It's darker inside the rooms, at this time of year, with the net curtains drawn. Your mother never would understand it. "Does old Masi keep them like that?" I used to ask her. "With the work he does, he'd be switching on the lights at two o'clock in the winter."'

'It's for you to say the word,' I told her.

I had grasped the two shafts and pushed the handcart forward. It was easy to move, as I'd expected. Grandmother was clasping the portrait to her breast, walking alongside of me. She didn't look back any more, on the contrary she walked faster and drew level with the cart, resting her hand on it to protect the load. In this manner we departed from our street for the new one, downhill, going down via de' Gondi, crossing a short stretch of the Piazza della Signoria, hugging close to the houses.

Ancora pochi minuti prima avevo riflettuto che via de' Gondi era in discesa, che non sarei stato capace di trattenere il carico da solo e che mi sarebbe convenuto, pure allungando il cammino, di passare dietro Badia,[14] per via del Proconsolo e piazza Sanfirenze; poi, l'atteggiamento della nonna, turbato com'ero dalle sue parole, mi aveva distratto. E fu come se via de' Gondi mi apparisse davanti all'improvviso, appena voltato l'angolo, inattesa.

Subito il carico mi prese la mano, le stanghe mi spezzavano i polsi, slittai, ma riuscii a tenermi forte alle stanghe, il corpo piegato sulla catenella che le congiungeva, quindi fu un volo, assurdo e nondimeno rispondente a una legge fisica qualsiasi: il carico mi trascinava e io sapevo mantenerlo diritto, in corsa, in equilibrio, al punto da inclinarlo per planare, non c'è altra parola, su via dei Leoni,[15] miracolosamente libera di passanti, di auto, di tram, fino a tentare ancora, raggiunto il piano, la voltata di via del Corno. Qui la ruota sinistra andò ad incastrarsi tra piedistallo e bandone del monumentino, lo divelse, il carico si rovesciò, le corde cedettero, e la nostra miseria si sciolse sul lastricato. La gente di via del Corno accorse, mi rialzò e mi sostenne, il maniscalco fu pronto col suo secchio d'acqua, una donna si fece largo sventolando un asciugamano, prima che arrivasse la nonna e mi si accasciasse a lato. Qualcuno pensò di raccogliere le sedie, ora che ci servivano ad entrambi, già l'incidente suscitava l'allegria. Incolume ma stordito, tardavo a rendermi conto del gran movimento.

«Il ragazzo, sbucciature,[16] e la vecchia meglio di prima» gridò una voce verso l'alto.

«Sono i nuovi inquilini del Carresi.»

«Nulla di grave, hanno soltanto deragliato.»

E già il nostro carico era di nuovo in piedi, completo di tutte le cianfrusaglie uscite dai cassetti dell'armadio, già la nonna spiegava che la signora del

Just a few minutes previously I had been reflecting that via de' Gondi ran downhill, that I wouldn't be able to control the load by myself and that it would suit me better, although it would make our way longer, to go behind the Badia, along via del Proconsolo and across Piazza Sanfirenze; but then grandmother's behaviour, disturbed as I was by her words, had distracted me. And via de' Gondi seemed to come upon me without warning, unexpectedly, scarcely had we turned the corner.

Suddenly the load went out of control. The shafts were breaking my wrists, and I slithered but managed to hold on tightly to the shafts, my body doubled over the small chain which linked them, and thereafter it became a flight, absurd but nonetheless responding to some kind of physical law: the load was dragging me along and I was managing to keep it on a straight course, on an even keel, to the point of steering it to go gliding, there's no other word for it, up via dei Leoni, miraculously free of passers-by, cars, trams – until the final attempt, once more on level ground, to take the corner into via del Corno. At this point the left wheel went and jammed itself between the base and the metal screen of the little monument, uprooting it, the load turned over, the ropes broke, and all our poverty spilled over the pavement. The inhabitants of via del Corno came running up, set me on my feet and supported me. The smith was ready with his bucket of water, and a woman made her way through waving a towel, before grandmother arrived on the scene and sank down at my side. Someone thought of picking up the chairs, which by now we were both glad to sit on, and already the incident was causing merriment. Unhurt but stunned, I was slow to appreciate all the commotion.

'The boy's a bit grazed, and the old woman's better than before,' shouted a voice to someone above.

'They're Carresi's new tenants.'

'It's nothing serious, they only came off the rails a bit.'

And already our load was upright again, complete with all the junk which had tumbled out of the cupboard drawers; already grandmother was explaining that the lady in

la fotografia era la sua figliola, la madre del ragazzo, già gradiva un goccio di vinsanto[17] per rimettersi dall'emozione. Una donna le diceva:

«Dalla sua camera, l'orologio di Palazzo Vecchio le sembrerà di averlo sul comodino.»

the photograph was her daughter, the boy's mother; already she was gladly accepting a drop of sweet wine to help her recover from the excitement. A woman was saying to her:

'In your room it'll seem as if you have the clock of the Palazzo Vecchio on your bedside table.'

HOUSES

CESARE PAVESE

Translated by Alexander Fainberg

LE CASE

Sono un uomo solo che lavora, e tutte le settimane aspetto la domenica. Non dico che questo giorno mi piaccia, ma faccio festa come tutti perché un riposo ci vuole. Una volta, quand'ero ancora ragazzo, pensai che, se avessi lavorato[1] anche la domenica, sarei diventato uomo piú presto degli altri, e mi feci dare la chiave dell'officina. Tutte le macchine erano ferme, ma io preparavo il lavoro del lunedí in poco tempo, e poi giravo nello stanzone vuoto, tendendo l'orecchio[2] e godendomela. Mi piaceva specialmente che potevo andarmene quando volevo e non facevo come i miei colleghi che in quell'ora giravano in bicicletta, all'osteria o in collina.

Anche adesso la gente alla domenica va fuori di città. Le vie si vuotano come un'officina. Io passo il pomeriggio camminandoci, e ce ne sono di quelle dove in mezz'ora non si vede un'anima. Sembra che tetti, marciapiedi e muri, e qualche volta i giardini, siano stati fatti soltanto per un uomo come me, che ci passa e ripassa e se li guarda venire incontro e allontanarsi, come succede delle colline e degli alberi in campagna.

C'è sempre qualche via piú vuota di un'altra. Alle volte mi fermo a guardarla bene, perché in quell'ora, in quel deserto, non mi pare di conoscerla. Basta che il sole, un po' di vento, il colore dell'aria siano cambiati, e non so piú dove mi trovo. Non finiscono mai, queste vie. Non par vero che tutte abbiano i loro inquilini e passanti, e che tutte se ne stiano cosí zitte e vuote. Piú che quelle lunghe e alberate della periferia dove potrei respirare un po' d'aria buona, mi piace girare le piazze e le viuzze del centro, dove ci sono i palazzi, e che mi sembrano ancora piú mie, perché

HOUSES

I am a man who keeps to himself and goes to work, and every week I look forward to Sunday. I can't say I like the day, but I take it off like everyone else because one must have a rest. Once, when I was still a boy, I thought if I worked on Sundays as well I should grow up to be a man more quickly than other people, and I got them to give me the key to the workshop. All the machines were still, but I got Monday's work ready in no time and then wandered about the huge empty place with my ears pinned back, enjoying myself. What I liked specially was that I could go just when I wanted to, and that I wasn't doing what my mates were doing at that moment, riding their bikes either on their way to the pub or up the hill.

People still go out of town on Sundays nowadays. The streets empty like a workshop. I spend the afternoon walking about, and there are some streets where you don't see a soul for half an hour. Roofs, pavements and walls, and sometimes the gardens, seem to have been made just for someone like me, who comes and goes and sees them coming closer and then getting away again, just as you do with hills and trees in the country.

There's always some street that is emptier than others. At times I stop and have a good look because at that hour, in that desert, I don't seem to recognize it. It's enough for the sun, a slight breeze, the colour of the air to have changed and I don't know where I am any more. They never end, these streets. It doesn't seem true that they should have all these people living there and passing by, and yet be so quiet and empty. Rather than walk about the long tree-lined streets on the outskirts where I could have a breath of good air I prefer to keep to the squares and lanes in the centre of the town where there are the large man-

proprio non si capisce come tutti se ne siano andati.

È successo con gli anni che non cerco piú compagnia come facevo una volta. Ma le domeniche allora erano un giorno diverso dagli altri. C'era di bello allora che ci si diceva: – Vieni quest'oggi nel tal posto, – e ci andavamo discorrendo. Si facevano strade nuove, si finiva in qualche cortile: io mi voltavo per riconoscermi e non sempre ci riuscivo. Ciccotto aveva la mia età, ma era a lui che piaceva girare nei cortili vuoti e salire delle scale dove non era mai salito, suonare alla porta e attaccare discorso con chi apriva. Io gli andavo dietro, e a quel tempo non credevo che suonasse a certe porte per la prima volta. Se l'avessi creduto, non sarei salito con lui. Aveva un'arte, specialmente se ci aprivano donne e bambini, di dire qualcosa che voleva risposta, e di parola in parola entravamo in casa scherzando e ci stavamo fino a sera. Diceva che la gente alla domenica s'annoia, e che chi da mezzo pomeriggio è chiuso in casa e non sente e non vede nessuno è ben contento di discorrere con chiunque. Io credo che di certe donne, che ci davano anche da bere, lui s'informasse prima.

Quegli anni c'era chi andava in barca, chi prendeva la bicicletta e si fermava soltanto all'osteria, chi aspettava le ragazze davanti al cinema. Da quando conobbi Ciccotto, queste cose mi parvero stupide e non osavo piú farle né parlargliene. Con lui, se si raccontava una cosa, non bastava che fosse capitata, bisognava che gli andasse a sangue;³ e ascoltava guardando in terra, con la faccia di chi ride di tutt'altro. Siccome era piccolotto e quasi gobbo, dispiaceva umiliarlo, e cosí succedeva che dipendevo da lui.

sions, squares, and lanes that seem to belong to me still more because it really doesn't seem possible that everybody should be gone.

With the years it has come about that I no longer look for company as I once used to. But in those days Sunday was a very different day from the others. Those were the days when we used to say, Come along to such and such a place today, and we would make our way there, talking all the time. We used to pick different roads and end up in some courtyard, and I would turn round to collect myself and see where I was though I didn't always succeed. Ciccotto and I were the same age but he was the one who liked to walk about the empty courtyards and climb stairs he had never climbed before, ring the bell and get into conversation with whoever opened the door. I used to walk behind him, and at the time I didn't believe that he rang at certain doors for the first time. Had I believed that he did I shouldn't have come up with him. He had a way with him, especially if the people who opened the door were women and children, to say something that called for a reply, then one word led to another and we would walk in joking and stay there till the evening. He used to say people were bored on Sundays, and that someone cooped up in the house half the afternoon without hearing or seeing anyone was quite pleased to talk to anybody. I think that about some women, those who gave us drinks as well, he found out beforehand.

In those years some of the boys went boating, others got on their bikes and only stopped at the pub, and others again waited for the girls in front of the cinema. Ever since I got to know Ciccotto these things seemed silly to me and I no longer had the heart to do them or talk to him about them. With him, when you told him something, it wasn't enough that it had happened, it had to be something he could feel and accept; he would listen with his eyes on the ground and a face as if he laughed at everybody else. Since he was pretty short and almost a hunchback it didn't seem right to hurt his feelings and so I came to depend on him.

LE CASE

C'erano case dove entrava chiedendo degli inquilini di prima e raccontando che venivamo apposta da fuori Quando una donna grassa ci apriva, le raccontava che in passato in quell'alloggio lui aveva abitato e ne era sperso.⁴ Altre volte voleva affittare e si faceva condurre dappertutto, fin sul balcone. Diceva che lo mandava il portinaio. Non gli piacevano le case dove stavano ragazze giovani.

Gli uomini, la sera, sono tutti all'osteria, ma uomini o donne che venissero ad aprire, il gioco gli riusciva sempre e scendevamo la scala ridendo. Nel discorso Ciccotto la vinceva lui, e le donne grasse che non escono e se ne stanno alla finestra a rinfrescarsi, ci dicevano sulla porta di tornare a trovarle la domenica dopo.

Ci tornavamo. Ma a nostro gusto, uno due mesi dopo. A Ciccotto piaceva capitare in un momento che la nostra conoscenza non fosse piú sola, avesse la famiglia, una vicina, dei conoscenti in casa, e allora intratteneva tutti, si metteva a scherzare, faceva star sulle spine la donna, chiedeva da bere lodando la bella accoglienza dell'altra volta. Finiva sempre che la donna lo prendeva da parte e gli faceva gli occhiacci, gli gridava qualcosa, aveva una crisi di soffoco. E Ciccotto era il primo a slacciarle il vestito.

Ridevo con Ciccotto tornando a casa ma non sapevo perché ridessi. Mi sentivo piú leggero, piú libero, come quando si esce dal teatro; lasciavo che Ciccotto parlasse, parlavo anch'io, ci piaceva indovinare i misteri e i pasticci di quella gente, inventarci le storie piú strambe, ma insomma ero contento che fosse finita. Forse ridevo proprio per questo, e solo per ingenuità aiutavo Ciccotto. Lui che in officina faceva il turno di notte, aveva per divertirsi anche la mattina dei giorni feriali, e certe conoscenze le coltivava allora per godersele meglio. A me che discutevo sovente, diceva che dovevo ancora girarne di case⁵ per conoscere le donne d'età. —

At some houses he went in and asked for former tenants, telling people we came specially from out of town. When a fat woman opened the door to us he told her he had lived there at one time and was still very fond of the place. Other times he wanted to rent the house and got them to show him all round the place, even up to the balcony. He said the porter had sent him. He did not like houses where there were young girls.

The men are usually all at the pub of an evening, but whether it was men or women who came to open the door, his game always came off and we used to go down the steps laughing. Ciccotto was always master of the conversation, and those fat women who don't go out and stand at the window to cool off told us at the door to come back to see them the following Sunday.

We did come back. But in our own good time, a month or two later. Ciccotto liked to turn up at a time when our acquaintance was no longer by herself, when she had her family about the place, or a neighbour, or some friends, and he would then entertain them all, begin to make jokes, keep the woman on tenterhooks and ask for a drink, praising the wonderful reception we had had the other day. In the end the woman always took him aside and made angry eyes at him, screamed something at him and worked herself up until she choked. And Ciccotto was there first to loosen her dress.

I used to laugh with Ciccotto when we went home but I didn't know why I laughed. I felt lighter, freer, as you do when you come out of the theatre. I let Ciccotto talk, and I talked, too. We liked to imagine the secrets of those people and their troubles, and to think up the oddest stories, but on the whole I used to be glad it was all over. Perhaps I laughed just because it was and only helped Ciccotto in my innocence. As he did the nightshift at the works he also had the weekday mornings to amuse himself in, and there were some acquaintances he cultivated then to enjoy himself even better. I often used to argue and he would say there were still a lot of houses for me to get round to so as to get to

Sei un ragazzo, – diceva; – non lo sai che i ragazzi sono i piú cercati?

Ma, per convincermi che ero un ragazzo, non mi portò dalla sua tabaccaia del pianterreno (avevamo attaccato discorso sotto la finestra una sera; faceva tanto caldo che lei aveva spento la luce e ci chiese di andarle a prendere il gelato; ci andai io. Ciccotto rimase sotto a parlarle). Salimmo invece una scala di quelle viuzze del centro che una volta erano palazzi e adesso sembrano cantine. C'era un cortile silenzioso e su per la scala che pareva scavata nella pietra mi fermai a guardare il cielo dalle finestrette. Fin lassú era arrivato Ciccotto. Ci stavano le cameriere di un palazzo che aveva il portone su un'altra strada. Ci aprí una ragazza con cappello e borsetta che gridò: – Caterina! – e senza dirci una parola ci passò in mezzo e scese la scala. Ciccotto era già entrato, parlava; io guardai dietro a lei, tanto m'era piaciuta. Non chiesi a Ciccotto chi fosse, perché avevo paura che la richiamasse e le facesse chi sa che discorso, ma entrai contento in una casa di dove uscivano ragazze simili.

Caterina era la solita donnetta grassa che piaceva a Ciccotto, e ci fermammo tutti e tre in una stanza che prendeva luce dal soffitto. Aspettai che parlassero, ma Ciccotto s'era buttato in poltrona e si guardava le unghie; Caterina sedette appoggiando i gomiti al tavolo. In un angolo sotto un'arcata buia c'era un letto disfatto.

– Siamo povere serve, – disse Caterina guardandomi.

Borbottai che la stanza era comoda e tutta per loro. Caterina scosse il capo e levando gli occhi all'insú disse che a volte ci pioveva. Feci una smorfia per divertirla, ma Ciccotto che ci osservava disse qualcosa non ricordo, forse «Muoviti» o «Non ci da' nulla?». e la donna si alzò di sussulto, girò indecisa per la stanza, pareva scontenta o assonnata; poi andò verso il letto, cercò in

know the older women. 'You are a boy,' he said, 'don't you know that boys are most sought after?'

But he didn't take me along to his tobacconist woman on the ground floor to convince me that I was a boy (we had started talking under the window one evening; it was so hot that she had put out the light and asked us to fetch her some ice-cream; I went. Ciccotto stayed below to talk to her.) Instead we went up a flight of steps in one of those lanes in the centre where there were mansions once which now look like cellars. There was a quiet courtyard and I stopped on the steps, which seemed cut into the stone, to look at the sky through the small windows. Ciccotto went right up there. It was where the maids lived of a mansion which had its front door opening on another road. A girl with hat and bag opened the door to us and shouted: 'Caterina!' Then, without saying a word, she passed between us and went down the steps. Ciccotto had already walked in and was talking. I looked back after her, I liked her so much. I didn't ask Ciccotto who she was because I was afraid he might call her back and say to her I don't know what, but I happily went into the house from which girls who looked like her were coming out.

Caterina was the usual fat little woman that Ciccotto liked, and we stopped all three of us in a room lit through skylights. I waited for them to speak, but Ciccotto had thrown himself into an armchair and was looking at his nails. Caterina sat down and propped her elbows on the table. An unmade bed stood in a corner, under a dark archway. 'We are only poor slaveys,' said Caterina, looking at me.

I muttered that the room was comfortable and that they had it all to themselves. Caterina shook her head, looked up and said that at times the rain came in. I pulled a face to amuse her but Ciccotto who was watching us said something, I don't remember what, perhaps 'Get a move on' or 'Won't you give us something?' and the woman got up with a start, walked undecidedly about the room and seemed unhappy, or perhaps sleepy; then she went over to

37

un comodino e tornò con un pacchetto di sigarette, a carta d'argento, che mi tese, e siccome esitavo, lo posò aperto sul tavolo. Ciccotto intanto si era alzato e accostato a una porta chiusa, e pareva ascoltasse. Caterina, buttato il pacchetto, sussultò come volesse dir qualcosa e si trattenne a stento. Ciccotto, voltandosi, la colse in quel gesto, ma mi sembrò non farne caso, venne invece al tavolo, si prese una sigaretta e l'accese. Allora Caterina disse: – Aspettatemi: torno, – aprí quella porta e corse via.

Nel tempo che stemmo soli – un momento – Ciccotto mi guardò come chi è lí per ridere, ma non rideva. – Non ho mai visto le finestre nel soffitto, – dissi. Lui guardò in su, ma pensava a tutt'altro. – Hai capito? – mi chiese. Per non offenderlo dissi: – Sta' attento – In quel momento rientrò Caterina. Ciccotto alzò le spalle. Caterina tornava con una bottiglia di liquore, che posò sul tavolo. Andò a cercare in un armadio tre bicchieri e li riempí adagio, voltandosi a invitarci con un sorriso franco. Bevemmo tutti e tre, e Ciccotto schioccò la lingua.[6] Allora anche Caterina si fece accendere la sigaretta e sedette fumando e facendosi vento. Discorremmo per un pezzo e Ciccotto la stuzzicava chiedendole se aveva molte visite, giacché teneva le sigarette e i liquori. Caterina non era una stupida e ribatteva con vivacità. Cosí, con le gambe accavallate, non sembrava una serva. Mi accorsi che nel momento ch'era uscita dalla stanza, s'era cambiata la gonna, e anche le labbra le aveva piú rosse. Ciccotto la fece parlare dei suoi tempi, e ne dissero tante. Io la stavo a sentire sbalordito. Caterina doveva essere stata la moglie o la donna di gran signori: parlava di quando le venivano in casa gli amici e l'orchestra e ballavano tutte le sere. Bevevamo ridendo. Ciccotto si guardò intorno una volta e borbottò: – Non ci sentono qui? – Caterina alzò le

the bed, searched in a bedside table and came back with a packet of cigarettes, wrapped in tinfoil, which she held out to me, and as I hesitated she put it open on the table. In the meantime Ciccotto had got up and gone over to a closed door; he seemed to be listening. Caterina, who had just tossed down the packet, started, as if she wanted to say something and held herself back with difficulty. Ciccotto turned round and caught her at it but as far as I could see he took no notice. He went over to the table instead, helped himself to a cigarette and lit it: Caterina then said: 'Wait – I'll be back in a minute.' She opened the very door he'd been at and went out.

While we were on our own – just for a moment – Ciccotto looked at me as if he was going to laugh, but he didn't. I said 'I never noticed the skylights'. He looked up but his mind was elsewhere. 'Got the idea?' he asked. I didn't want to hurt him, so I said: 'Watch out.' Just then Caterina came in again. Ciccotto shrugged.

Caterina came back with a bottle of liquor and put it on the table. She fetched three glasses from a cupboard, filled them slowly, and turned round to invite us with a frank smile. We all drank and Ciccotto clicked his tongue to show he liked it. Then Caterina also got a light for her cigarette and sat down, smoking and fanning herself.

We talked for a while and Ciccotto teased her. He asked her whether she had many visitors, seeing that she had cigarettes and liquor handy. Caterina was no fool and answered back smartly. The way she was sitting, with her legs crossed, she did not look like a slavey. I noticed that while she had been out of the room she had changed her skirt and put some more red on her lips. Ciccotto made her tell about her life, and they didn't stop talking about it. I sat and listened. Caterina must have been the wife or the lady of great gentlemen. She talked about the times she had had friends come to see her, and she had an orchestra in, and they danced every single night. We drank and laughed. Once Ciccotto looked round and muttered: 'Can't they hear

spalle tutta incalorita e rispose che non c'era nessuno.

Mi chiedevo perché Ciccotto avesse avuto quel riguardo. Intanto il discorso voltò sui padroni, e Ciccotto le chiese se la vedova si era sposata. – T'interessa? – ribatté Caterina con tutt'altra faccia. Ciccotto rideva. Io allora chiesi da quanto tempo si conoscevano, e Ciccotto cominciò a raccontare. Raccontando guardava lei, malizioso. Disse che un giorno era comparsa in quella stanza la padrona, la vedova, una domenica che la casa era vuota (Caterina arrossí e si agitò), che li aveva trovati in quel letto, e senza spaventarsi aveva detto a lui di vestirsi in sua presenza, e lui l'avrebbe fatto ma Caterina gli tirava le coperte sulla testa, con quel caldo: gelosa come tutte le donne. Io stavo a sentire guardandolo, per non guardare Caterina, e dissi: – Poi ti sei vestito?

Qui Caterina, esasperata, gridò: – Tu! Ti vestivi sicuro. Non è la faccia che ti manca –. Ciccotto rideva. Caterina s'era coperta la faccia con le mani.

Io lo giuro che volevo andarmene. Ma invece guardavo quella porta, e non sapevo che dire. Ciccotto si alzò per versarsi da bere. Al movimento, Caterina levò la testa – rossa con gli occhi enormi, sembrava volesse sbranarlo. – Va' di là, va' di là, non è uscita, – gridò a voce bassa. – È piú sporca di te che sei venuto a cercarla.

Ciccotto finí di versare e posò la bottiglia. Stette un momento come incerto, soprapensiero. Poi ritornò a sedersi e disse a me: – Queste donne non escono mai.

Caterina ci guardava, ancora sussultante. – Dovrebbe darvi una finestra, – osservò Ciccotto. – Una finestra sulla strada. Ne ha tante –. Caterina alzò le spalle, scon-

us here?' Caterina, who had quite warmed up by then, shrugged her shoulders; there was no one there, she said.

I wondered why Ciccotto had been careful like that. Meanwhile the talk turned to employers and Ciccotto asked her whether the widow had got married. 'Are you interested?' Caterina snapped back with an entirely different expression on her face. Ciccotto laughed. I then asked how long they had known each other and Ciccotto began to tell me. While he was talking he looked at her, slyly. He said one day the mistress, the widow, had turned up in the room, one Sunday when the house was empty (Caterina blushed and fidgeted), that she had found them in that bed over there, that she hadn't been shocked at all, and had told him to get dressed in her presence. He would have done so but Caterina had pulled the covers over his head, in that heat as well: jealous like all women. I sat there listening and watching him so as not to look at Caterina, and I said: 'Did you get dressed then?'

That was when Caterina got mad at him and cried out, 'You got dressed all right, you! If you are short of anything at all it certainly isn't nerve.' Ciccotto laughed. Caterina had covered her face with her hands.

I swear I wanted to go. But instead I looked at that door and didn't know what to say. Ciccotto got up to pour himself a drink. When she saw him move Caterina lifted her face – red and with enormous eyes, she looked as if she wanted to tear him to pieces. 'Get away from there, get away, she hasn't gone out,' she cried softly, 'she is even dirtier than you are, looking for her!'

Ciccotto finished pouring and put the bottle down. He stood for a moment as if uncertain, absent-minded. Then he went back to his seat and said to me: 'These women never go out.'

Caterina looked at us, still fidgety. 'One should give you a window,' remarked Ciccotto, 'a window on the street. After all the house has so many.' Caterina shrugged her

trosa. – Quella non sta alle finestre, – disse ancora Ciccotto; – non ne ha bisogno.

Caterina borbottò qualcosa. Si asciugò la bocca col fazzoletto e guardava me. Sembrava che l'avesse con me. Feci il gesto di alzarmi e volevo dire: – Sarà meglio che vada, – quando lei saltò in piedi e mi offrí un altro bicchierino.

Non trovai le parole e restai. Caterina adesso taceva offesa, e Ciccotto ci guardava tranquillo. La stanza era piena di luce.

– Ecco, – disse Ciccotto, – dovrebbe tornare la Lina. Sono giovani e andrebbero d'accordo.

Dal discorso capii che la Lina era l'altra ragazza, quella ch'era uscita entrando noi. Caterina disse che l'altra stava sí alla finestra e che era sfacciata. – Ma la Lina a lui piace, – disse Ciccotto – Lui non sa quel che è buono –. Io guardavo il mio bicchiere e tendevo l'orecchio. Mi era venuta una speranza. Ma non si sentivano passi.

Chiesi quando tornava la Lina. – Voi dovete parlare, – dissi. – Io non c'entro –. Questa volta mi ero alzato e ci riuscivo. Caterina mi ficcò in tasca delle sigarette perché finissi il pomeriggio. Feci la scala senza voltarmi, e solo in piazza respirai.

Fu quello il primo pomeriggio che girai per la città vuota. L'idea che adesso conoscevo Lina, e che in quel momento Ciccotto faceva all'amore mi agitava, mi esaltava. Ero un poco ubriaco. Ero giovane, e tutto mi sembrava cosí facile. Non sapevo ancora ch'ero contento perché solo.

Quella sera, mentre aspettavo Ciccotto in piazza, guardai la finestra della sua tabaccaia, e me la risi. Ciccotto era proprio canaglia. Poi, quando arrivò, chiacchierammo di tutto. Mi spiegò quel che fanno e che dicono le donne gelose. Mi disse che al mondo non sanno far altro, tant'è vero che passano il tempo alla finestra, magari dietro le persiane. Bisogna conoscerle, e un gio-

shoulders in a temper. 'She doesn't stand at the window,' Ciccotto went on, 'she doesn't need to.'

Caterina muttered something. She wiped her mouth with her handkerchief and looked at me. She seemed angry with me. I made as if to get up and was going to say 'I'd better go', when she jumped to her feet and offered me another glass.

I couldn't find the words and stayed. Caterina was hurt now and didn't say a word; Ciccotto calmly looked at us. The room was full of light.

'Well, Lina should be back by now,' said Ciccotto. 'They are young and they'd be quite a good match.'

From the conversation I understood that Lina was the other girl, the one that went out when we came in. Caterina said that the other girl did stand at the window, and that she was a hussy. 'But he is keen on Lina,' said Ciccotto. 'He doesn't know what's good for him.' I looked at my glass and my ears were flapping. I began to hope. But we didn't hear any steps.

I asked when Lina would be back. 'You'll want to talk,' I said, 'and it's none of my business.' This time I had managed to get up. Caterina pushed some cigarettes into my pocket so that I would have enough to last me the afternoon. I went down the steps without turning round and only breathed again when I was in the square.

That was the first afternoon I spent roaming about the empty city. The thought that I now knew Lina, and that at that moment Ciccotto was making love, stirred and excited me. I was a little drunk. I was young, and everything seemed so easy to me. I didn't know yet that I was happy because I was alone.

That evening, while I waited for Ciccotto in the square, I looked at the tobacconist woman's window and laughed. Ciccotto was a proper scoundrel. Afterwards, when he came we talked about it all. He explained to me what jealous women do and say. He told me that they can't help it, that's why they spend their time at the window, perhaps behind the shutters. One had to get to know them, and a young lad

vanotto le conosce a ogni modo. Viene un'età, diceva, che lo aspettano dietro la porta come le gatte.

Ma adesso pensava alla sua tabaccaia e non voleva piú salire da Caterina. Mi disse di andarci solo, magari di sera. Io non ebbi il coraggio. Gironzolai sotto i balconi del palazzo, sperando di vedere la Lina affacciata. Ma le vetrate erano chiuse; tutto il mattino della domenica successiva restarono chiuse, e fu Ciccotto che mi disse che d'estate tutta quanta la famiglia andava al mare. – Anche le serve ? – Anche loro.

Non capivo: Caterina era tanto gelosa, e una settimana prima di andarsene non ne aveva parlato. – Sono cosí, le donne, – disse Ciccotto.

Lui non era piú l'uomo di prima: non faceva piú il gioco di tornare con me per le scale dove si era cominciato a ridere. Non si staccava dalla piazza, passava tutte le domeniche intorno alla tabaccheria. La tabaccaia era l'unica donna che non lo lasciasse entrare in casa; gli parlava, anche di sera, dalla finestra del pianterreno, lo mandava a prenderle il gelato; stavano zitti delle mezze ore ascoltando morire i passi di chi traversava. Questa donna aveva forse trent'anni, ma sembrava ne avesse quaranta, tanto sapeva comandare e dar risposta.

Io, da solo, far la vita di prima non c'ero tagliato. Mi accontentavo di vedere Ciccotto all'officina; e andavo a spasso, mi ero fatto qualche collega, sapevo ancora divertirmi, ma non ero piú quello. Si sa com'è in casa: se uno dorme di giorno, lo svegliano, e poi da casa all'officina dall'officina a casa non è piú un vivere. Cominciai quell'estate a girare da solo, tutto il tempo che avevo, le strade e le piazze, e passare per quelle viuzze e cercare la Lina che invece era al mare. Speravo, non so come, di vedermela un giorno spuntare davanti. Quando le vie sono deserte, tutto può succedere. Mi fermavo sugli angoli.

got to know them in any case. There comes a time, he said, when they wait for him behind the door like cats.

But right now he was thinking of his tobacconist woman and he didn't want to go up to Caterina's any more. He told me to go there by myself, perhaps of an evening. I didn't dare. I mooched along under the balconies of the mansion, hoping to see Lina at the window. But the windows were closed. They stayed closed all through the morning of the following Sunday, and it was Ciccotto who finally told me that, come the summer, the whole family went to the seaside, bag and baggage. 'Even the slaveys?' 'Yes, of course.'

I didn't understand it: Caterina was so jealous, and she hadn't said a word about it a week before she went. 'There's a woman for you,' said Ciccotto.

He was no longer the man he used to be. He no longer played the game of coming back with me along the steps where we used to start laughing. He didn't budge from the square and spent every Sunday round the tobacconist's shop. The tobacconist was the only woman who didn't let him into the house, she talked to him, also of an evening, from the ground floor window, and sent him out to fetch her ice-cream. They were quiet for half an hour at a time listening to the steps of passers-by fading away. The woman was thirty perhaps, but she seemed to be forty from the way she ordered him about and answered him.

On my own I wasn't cut out to lead our former life. It was enough for me to see Ciccotto at work, and I went for walks, I had got myself some pals, I still knew how to enjoy myself, but I was no longer the same. You know how it is at home; if you sleep during the day they wake you up. And then to go straight from home to work, and then straight back home again isn't living any more. That summer I began to wander about the roads and squares on my own, every minute that I could spare, to walk along the lanes and look for Lina who was at the seaside all the while. I was hoping, I don't know how, to see her spring up suddenly in front of me one day. When the streets are deserted anything may happen. I would stop at the corners.

E poi, non c'era solo la Lina. Ciccotto ne conosceva
tante, di donne. Viene un'età che ti corrono dietro,
lo diceva sempre. Di salire le scale, di farle parlare,
di cercare, d'insistere, d'innamorarle, non ero capace.
Ci riusciva Ciccotto, ch'era quasi gobbo; io sapevo che
bastava aspettare.

Ma poi Ciccotto si sposò. Non me lo disse nemmeno;
lo seppi da mia sorella. La tabaccaia lo faceva venir
matto, e sposarla fu l'unico modo per entrarle in casa.
Lui fino alla fine non mi disse mai altro se non ch'era
troppo gelosa, ch'era una bella donna grassa e se a me
non piaceva. – Per prendere in giro[7] una donna, – diceva,
– bisogna non dargliela vinta –. La sposò quasi di nascosto perché lei era vedova e gli diceva sempre che
rimaritandosi avrebbe perduto i clienti. Ma, appena
maritata, mise lui dietro il banco. Io allora risi di Ciccotto, come tutti ne risero, e finí che litigammo e ci
vedemmo soltanto quando passavo sulla piazza. Ma
adesso ci sono dei giorni, qualche domenica, che lo
invidio.

And after all there was not only Lina. Ciccotto knew women, so many of them. There comes a time when they run after you, he always used to say. Whatever it was – climbing the steps, making them talk, seeking them out, urging them on, charming them – I couldn't do it. Ciccotto could, almost hunchbacked as he was; I knew it was enough just to wait.

But then Ciccotto got married. He didn't even tell me; I heard it from my sister. The tobacconist woman drove him crazy, and marrying her was the only way to get into her place. In the finish he didn't tell me a thing any more except that she was too jealous, that she was a handsome plump woman and whether I didn't like her. To come off best with a woman, he said, you mustn't let her have her own way. He married her almost secretly because she was a widow and always told him that if she remarried she would lose her customers. But as soon as they were married she put him behind the counter. And then I laughed at Ciccotto, as everybody did, and in the end we quarrelled and only met when I passed through the square. But now there are days, some Sunday perhaps, when I envy him.

THE POOR
CARLO CASSOLA

Translated by Anthony Rhodes

I POVERI

Arrivata alla scaletta, si fermò un momento, come per darsi il coraggio sufficiente a compiere quella visita penosa. Il quartiere si stendeva sotto di lei con la sua selva di tettucci rossi, irti di abbaini e di comignoli. Sulla destra, era limitato dalle mura,[1] sulla sinistra, da una grande frana bianca di detriti d'alabastro, risalita trasversalmente da un sentierino.

Prima di iniziare la sua attività di Visitatrice, la signorina non ci aveva mai messo piede. Ora non c'era giorno, si può dire, che non si avventurasse in quel dedalo di vicoli e di scalette. L'inverno prima per il gelo era caduta, proprio in quel punto dove stava passando adesso, e s'era lussata una spalla. Le case erano quasi tutte senza intonaco; avevano finestre piccole, quadrate, con pentole e barattoli di gerani sui davanzali.

– Buonasera, signorina, – disse una donna seduta sullo scalino di una porta. Si teneva sulle ginocchia una bambina di cinque o sei anni.

La signorina si sentí in dovere di fermarsi:

– Come sta vostro marito? – chiese alla donna.

– Come vuole che stia? – rispose quella. Era bruna, ancor giovane, dalle forme piene: sarebbe stata una bella donna, se non avesse avuto il viso butterato. – Sono sei mesi che è fuori dal lavoro. Come si può stare, in queste condizioni?

– Ma di salute come sta?

– Di salute, starebbe discretamente[2] ... Alle volte la notte ha un po' di affanno.

– Quello non vi deve preoccupare, – disse la signorina. – Io vedo che gli alabastrai, dal piú al meno, un po' d'asma ce l'hanno tutti. L'essenziale è che non abbia piú avuto attacchi di cuore. Non ne ha piú avuti, vero?

THE POOR

On arriving at the little flight of steps she stopped for a moment, as if to summon up courage to make the difficult visit ahead. The district of the town extended below, a forest of little red roofs bristling with skylights and gables. On the right, it was bounded by the town walls; on the left, by a large white slope formed from pieces of rejected alabaster, up which a footpath ran diagonally.

Before starting her work as a Visitor, the signorina had never set foot here before. Now one might say that not a day passed without her venturing into this labyrinth of narrow streets and small steps. Last winter the surface had been frozen; at this very point where she was now walking, she had fallen and broken her shoulder. The houses were nearly all unplastered, with small square windows which had saucepans and tins of geraniums on the sills.

'Good evening, signorina,' said a woman sitting on the steps of a doorway. On her knees she held a small child, aged about five or six.

The signorina felt she must stop.

'How's your husband?' she asked.

'What do you expect?' replied the woman. She had a dark complexion and was still young and buxom; she might have been beautiful if her face had not been pock-marked. 'He's been out of work six months. How do you expect him to be, with all this?'

'But his health?'

'Oh, his health's all right. He occasionally has a little difficulty breathing at night.'

'I shouldn't worry too much about that,' said the signorina. 'Most alabaster workers seem to have a touch of asthma. The main thing is, he hasn't had any more heart attacks. He hasn't, has he?'

– No, quelli no – rispose la donna.

– Mi fa piacere – disse la signorina – Sapete, la salute è la prima cosa. Per il resto ... il Sïgnore provvede sempre.

– La salute è la prima cosa, ma anche il lavoro ... – Bruscamente la donna mise da parte la bambina e si alzò: – Sono sei mesi, capisce? che in casa nostra entrano solo i soldi del sussidio ...

– Sí, sí, capisco – si affrettò a dire la signorina.

– Ha fatto domanda da dieci parti, ma dappertutto ha avuto la stessa risposta. E sí che mio marito, lei lo conosce? non è per nulla esigente. Si adatterebbe a far qualsiasi lavoro, pur di portare il pane a casa.

– Neanche alla cooperativa dei boscaioli gli hanno dato speranza? – disse la signorina. – Io, ricordo, parlai col signor Puccianti, e mi promise ...

– Sí, sí, belle speranze gli hanno dato alla cooperativa. Prima di tutto, siamo nella stagione morta, e non c'è da pensare ad assumere nuovi operai. Bisogna lasciar passare l'estate, cosí gli hanno detto, e poi, in autunno, si vedrà. Già, e noi d'estate cosa si mangia? Sono queste le risposte da dare a un padre di famiglia? – La donna aveva alzato la voce: – Ma come si fa ad andare avanti in questo modo? Me lo dica lei, signorina, come si fa ad andare avanti? Ma cosa vogliono, che uno si metta a rubare per portare un tozzo di pane alla famiglia?

La signorina si era tirata leggermente indietro. La mettevano a disagio, quasi le incutevano paura quegli occhi spiritati, quella faccia pustolosa, quel tono di voce aspro. Dalla porta accanto s'era affacciata una donnetta, assisteva alla scena.

– Be' ... ora mi dispiace, ma devo andare, – disse finalmente la signorina. – Speriamo che vostro marito possa trovar lavoro presto.

– Lo so io cosa bisognerebbe sperare, – fece la donna cupa. La signorina aspettò ansiosa il seguito. – In un'epidemia, bisognerebbe sperare: in un'epidemia che

'No, not those,' replied the woman.

'I'm glad of that,' said the signorina. 'Health, you know, is the first thing. For everything else ... well, God always provides.'

'Health is the first thing – but so is work.' The woman abruptly put the child aside and got up. 'Don't you realize it's been going on for six months now? The only money coming into the house is from the public assistance ...'

'Yes, yes, I know ...' the signorina replied hastily.

'He's tried ten places. The same reply from all of them. And you know, my husband – he's not at all demanding. He'll do any work – if it brings in food for the family.'

'But surely, the Foresters' Cooperative held out some hope?' said the signorina. 'I remember, I spoke to Signor Puccianti, and he promised me ...'

'Yes, yes, fine hopes they gave him at the Cooperative. First, they said, it's the slack season and there's no question of taking on more hands. We'll wait until the summer's over, they said. And then – we'll think about it again in the autumn. Fine! Yes, and what are we going to eat during the summer? Is that the sort of reply you give the father of a family?' The woman had raised her voice. 'How are we going to manage like this? Just tell me, signorina, how are we going to manage? Do they want people to start stealing in order to get a scrap of bread for the family?'

The signorina had drawn back a little. The mad look in those eyes, that pock-marked face, that strident tone, made her feel uncomfortable, almost frightened. A little woman had appeared in the next doorway, from where she was watching the scene.

'Well, I'm sorry, I must go now,' said the signorina at last. 'Let's hope your husband soon finds a job.'

'Hope! Yes, we've got to hope a lot,' said the woman gloomily. The signorina waited anxiously for what she was going to say next. 'We must hope for an epidemic. An

ci levasse dal mondo, me, quel disgraziato del mio marito e questa creatura.

La signorina non poté frenare un moto di sollievo: aveva temuto che la donna uscisse fuori con qualche discorso sovversivo. Non sarebbe stata la prima volta che ne sentiva fare ad alta voce, in quel quartiere dove ogni tanto comparivano anche scritte sui muri. – Non dovete parlare cosí, – disse. – Bisogna sempre sperare nell'aiuto del Signore –. E riprendendo il tono autorevole che le era abituale: – Sentite una cosa, piuttosto: dove sta Chiorboli? Quel muratore che ha la moglie malata?

– Qui di sotto, – rispose la donna, che era ricaduta nell'indifferenza. – L'ultima casa del vicolo. Vai ad accompagnarla, Tatiana.

– Non importa, grazie, – si schermí la signorina; ma la bimba le s'era messa al fianco. Presero a destra per una scaletta, quindi imboccarono un vicolo cieco. La bimba la accompagnò fino alla porta:

– Sta al secondo piano, – disse, e svelta se ne tornò indietro.

– Grazie, cara, – fece la signorina.

Salí su per la scaletta buia. Al primo piano la porta era spalancata, si vedeva una cucina in disordine, con un bimbo di cinque o sei anni nudo in piedi su una sedia accostata all'acquaio; la madre lo stava lavando, il bimbo piagnucolava. «Potrebbero almeno chiudere la porta», pensò la signorina. Quello che piú la irritava nei poveri era la mancanza di pudore. Salí la seconda rampa e si trovò davanti a una porta. Al buio cercò il campanello o un battente, senza trovarlo; stava per chiamare, quando si accorse che la porta era soltanto socchiusa. La spinse ed entrò in una cucina, anch'essa al buio.

– Permesso, – disse. Le rispose una voce, o meglio un lamento. – Sono la signorina Verdi. Vengo da parte delle Visitatrici.

– Avanti, signorina, avanti, – piagnucolò la voce.

Tastoni la signorina attraversò la stanza e spinse una porta. Subito fu colpita da un odore acre di sudore e di

54

epidemic to kill us all off. Me – my wretched husband – and this creature here.'

The signorina could not help feeling a little relieved; she had feared the woman might come out with a subversive speech. It would not have been the first time people had spoken their minds in this part of the town, where writings of this kind sometimes appeared on the walls. 'You shouldn't talk like that,' she said. 'We must always hope for God's help.' And then, employing again her usual authoritative tone, 'And tell me, where's Chiorboli? The bricklayer with the sick wife.'

'There, down the street,' the woman became listless again. 'The last house. Go with her, Tatiana!'

'No, it doesn't matter, thank you,' parried the signorina; but the child was already at her side. They went off to the right down some small steps, and turned into a blind alley. The child accompanied her as far as the door.

'She's on the second floor,' it said, and then turned back briskly.

'Thank you, my dear,' said the signorina.

She went up the dark staircase. On the first floor, the door was wide open; she saw an untidy kitchen, with a five- or six-year-old child standing naked on a chair drawn up beside the sink; its mother was washing it and the infant was whining. 'They might at least shut the door,' thought the signorina. What annoyed her most about the poor was their lack of modesty. She climbed the second flight and found herself standing in front of a door. In the dark she groped for a bell or knocker, but without finding it; she was about to call out, when she realized that the door was only ajar. She pushed it and entered a kitchen, which was in darkness too.

'May I come in?' she said. A voice, or rather a groan answered her. 'I'm Signorina Verdi. I've come on behalf of the Visitors.'

'Come in, signorina! Come in!' whined the voice.

Groping, the signorina crossed the room and pushed open a door – to be suddenly assailed by an acrid smell of sweat

orina. Andò alla finestra e la spalancò. – Ah, – disse sollevata. – Un po' d'aria fa sempre bene, – aggiunse rivolta all'inferma.

Questa era una donna grassa, col faccione rosso sudato. Stava sollevata sul letto, con la schiena appoggiata a due cuscini senza le federe.

La signorina diede un'occhiata al lenzuolo, che era piuttosto sporco, quindi si rivolse alla donna:

– Quant'è che siete malata? – domandò.

– Un anno, – rispose la donna; – ma allettata proprio, un mese.

– E ora come vi sentite? Un po' meglio?

– Ma che dice, signorina; mi sembra di perdere le forze ogni giorno di piú. Le gambe le ho gonfie, se vedesse ... Se non c'è qualcuno che mi aiuta, non sono nemmeno capace di alzarmi per orinare.

– Si capisce, a stare a letto si diventa deboli. Chi è il vostro medico, il dottor Carboni? – L'inferma fece cenno di sí. – Cosa dice, quanto vi ci vorrà per rimettervi?

– Il dottore, senta, prima di tutto non viene mai; e quando viene, non dà per nulla soddisfazione.

La signorina le rivolse qualche altra domanda (ormai, con la sua doppia pratica di infermiera e di visitatrice, ne sapeva quanto un medico), quindi prese la scatola di iniezioni che era sul comodino e la considerò per un momento.

– Di queste, quante vi ha detto di farne? Una ogni giorno?

– Una ogni due giorni, – rispose l'inferma. – Viene a farmele una donna ...

– Ma chi vi assiste? Vostro marito, immagino, sarà sempre fuori per lavoro, ma non avete qualche persona ... che so, una sorella, una cognata?

– Ho una cognata, la moglie di mio fratello; ma si figuri, sta in campagna, ha quattro figlioli, non ha davvero il tempo di assistere me. Se ho bisogno di qualcosa, do una voce a questa famiglia di sotto. Ma

and urine. She went to the window and threw it open. 'Ah!' she turned, relieved, to the invalid. 'A little fresh air is always a good thing.'

The invalid was a fat woman with a large, red, sweating face. She was raised in the bed, her back propped up against two cushions without pillow-cases.

The signorina gave a glance at the dirty sheets and then addressed the woman.

'How long have you been ill?' she asked.

'A year,' replied the woman. 'But I've been completely bed-ridden for a month.'

'How do you feel now? A little better?'

'What do you expect, signorina? I seem to lose a little more strength every day. If you looked, you'd see my legs are swollen. If I'm not helped, I can't even get up to pass water.'

'Staying in bed makes you weaker, you know. Who's your doctor? Carboni?' The sick woman made an affirmative sign. 'What does he say – how long before you get well?'

'Listen. In the first place the doctor doesn't ever come. And secondly, when he does, he's absolutely no use.'

The signorina put a few more questions (with her double activity, as nurse and Visitor, she knew by now as much as a doctor); then she picked up a box of injections on the bedside table and examined it for a moment.

'How many of these does he say you're to have? One a day?'

'One every other day,' replied the invalid. 'A woman comes and gives them to me.'

'But who looks after you? Your husband's away at work all day, I suppose. Haven't you anybody else ... I mean, a sister, a sister-in-law?'

'I've a sister-in-law, my brother's wife. But, you see, she's always away in the country, she has four children. She certainly hasn't time for me. If I need anything, I call the family below. But I'm here all the time alone, signorina!

Io sto tutto il tempo sola, si immagini un po', signorina ... Sto qui sola, ad aspettare la morte ..., – e la donna cominciò a piangere chetamente.

– Via, non avvilitevi, – disse la signorina. – Il vostro stato non è grave, avete solo bisogno di un po' di compagnia per risollevarvi il morale. Ora mi dispiace che debbo andare, ma vi prometto di tornare presto a farvi una visita.

Quando fu arrivata in cima ai centotrenta scalini, la signorina emise un sospiro di sollievo. Non era solo il sollievo fisico che fosse finita la salita: era anche il sollievo spirituale che fosse finita la vista di quelle miserie.

Arrivata in chiesa, guardò subito verso il primo banco a sinistra, dove si metteva sempre la marchesa Lastrucci; e la vide infatti, col cappellino e la veletta; ma scorse anche la nobildonna[3] Ormanni, e allora sedette sulla prima panca libera, accanto a una donnetta dagli occhi rossi, che biascicava il rosario. Di lí a un minuto entrò il sacerdote, e la funzione ebbe inizio.

In ginocchio, col viso nascosto fra le mani, la signorina diceva una dopo l'altra le preghiere, ma il suo pensiero era altrove. Ripensava ai suoi poveri, e in un modo non proprio benevolo. Quella donna che aveva il marito disoccupato, tanto per cominciare, era tutta ingioiellata, «È cosí, sono zingari, quando il marito lavora e guadagna, spendono fino all'ultimo centesimo; non pensano a metter qualcosa da parte». Quanto all'inferma, su lei magari[4] non trovava nulla da ridire; ma possibile che la lasciassero in tale abbandono? Il marito, magari, finito il lavoro se ne andava all'osteria, invece di tornarsene a casa. E quella cognata che non s'era fatta viva una volta, in tutto il tempo della malattia?

Fuori di chiesa trovò la marchesa, che si era liberata della Ormanni. La marchesa si sorprese di vederla:

– Oh, – disse, – credevo che non fossi venuta. Sai, pensavo che avessi fatto tardi ...

Just think of it! I'm here alone, waiting to die ...' The woman began crying quietly.

'Now come, you mustn't let yourself get depressed,' said the signorina. 'Your condition isn't serious. All you need is a bit of company to raise your spirits. I'm sorry I must go now. But I promise to come back soon and see you.'

When the signorina arrived at the top of the hundred and thirty steps she heaved a sigh of relief, not only at having finished the climb, but with another kind of relief, spiritual relief, at having finished viewing such misery.

On entering the church she immediately looked round at the first row on the left, where the Marchesa Lastrucci always sat. Yes, she was there, in her little hat and veil. But she saw the Nobildonna Ormanni too; and then she sat down on the first free bench, beside a small red-eyed woman who was mumbling over her rosary. A minute later the priest appeared, and the service began.

On her knees, her face hidden in her hands, the signorina repeated the prayers one after the other; but her thoughts were elsewhere. She was thinking of her poor – and not very kindly. That woman with the out-of-work husband for one, she was all covered with jewellery. 'They're like that, they're gypsies. When the husband works and earns, they spend it down to the last farthing. They don't think of saving.' As for the invalid – well, there was nothing much she could say about her. But was it really possible that the woman could be left all alone like that? No doubt the husband would be off to the tavern when he'd finished work, instead of coming back home. And what about that sister-in-law who hadn't shown a sign of life once, throughout the whole illness?

Outside the church she found the Marchesa, who had got rid of Signora Ormanni. The Marchesa was surprised to see her. 'Ah!' she said. 'I thought you weren't coming. You see, I thought you were arriving late, because ...'

– No, no, sono arrivata in tempo. Ma ti ho vista con quella lí . . .

– Cosa c'è di nuovo? – la interruppe la Lastrucci.

– Nulla c'è di nuovo, cara Maria, – rispose la signorina con enfasi. – Sempre le solite cose, miserie, malattie, spettacoli di degradazione materiale e morale . . .

Rimasero ancora a parlare per qualche minuto, e la signorina ebbe modo di dire altre frasi alate; ma intanto non perdeva d'occhio la lattaia, che se ne stava sulla porta della bottega. Aveva capito che voleva parlarle, e aveva capito anche che si trattava di una raccomandazione per il cognato. Ma stasera era troppo stanca per ascoltarla. Perciò, appena la vide occupata con un avventore, si affrettò a prender congedo dall'amica. Si abbracciarono e si baciarono, come tutte le sere; quindi la marchesa, appoggiandosi al bastone, si avviò pesantemente verso la piazza. Dal canto suo la signorina entrò svelta nel portone.

Una volta in casa si cambiò, poi passò nella stanza che le serviva da ufficio, da salottino da lavoro e da sala da pranzo. Era una stanza piccola, e non certo piú allegra delle altre, perché dava su un cortiletto che era un vero e proprio pozzo, dove il sole non scendeva mai. Inoltre era la piú frigida della casa. Ma tant'è, in quella stanza la signorina passava le sue giornate. Il mobilio consisteva in uno scrittoio, una poltroncina di vimini, un'altra sedia, una credenza e due scaffali su cui erano allineati i pochi libri che la signorina possedeva: Vite di Santi, altri volumi di argomento religioso, e poi tutte le pubblicazioni del Touring Club, di cui era socia da molti anni. La signorina non aveva mai avuto l'abitudine di leggere molto. Viaggiare, questo sí, le sarebbe piaciuto; ma essendo sola, non se n'era potuto levare la voglia. Piú che altro aveva approfittato dei pellegrinaggi per vedere un po' di mondo. E durante la guerra, era stata infermiera a Salonicco.

Prima di cena, ebbe tempo di scrivere una lettera.

'No, no. I was on time. But I saw you with her, there . . .'

'Any news?' interrupted the Marchesa Lastrucci.

'No news, Maria dear,' replied the signorina emphatically. 'Always the same – poverty, sickness, scenes of moral and physical degradation . . .'

They went on talking for a while and the signorina had the chance of adding a number of similar high-sounding phrases about what she had seen. While they talked she could not help noticing the milk-woman who was standing at the door of her shop; she knew the woman wanted to speak to her, and she knew it was about a favour for her brother-in-law. But this evening she was too tired to listen to her; so, as soon as she saw the milk-woman engaged with a client, she quickly left her friend. They embraced and kissed, as they always did in the evening. Then the Marchesa, supporting herself on her stick, set off laboriously for the piazza. The signorina meanwhile went hurriedly under the big doorway.

Once home she changed and went into the room which served her as office, work-room, and dining-room; it was a small room, certainly no more cheerful than the others, for it gave onto a small courtyard, a veritable well into which the sunlight never fell. It was also the coldest room in the house. In spite of this, the signorina used to spend the day here. The furniture consisted of a writing-desk, a small wicker armchair, another chair, a sideboard and two shelves on which her few books were aligned: *Lives of the Saints* and other volumes of a religious nature, and all the publications of the Touring Club, of which she had been a member for many years. The signorina had never been much of a reader. Travel, yes, she would have liked to travel; but being on her own, she had never been able to satisfy the wish. Her pilgrimages had been particularly valuable for seeing a bit of the world; during the war she had been a nurse in Salonica.

She had time before supper to write a letter. After the

Dopo mangiato, sfilò dalla fascetta «L'Osservatore Romano»,[5] che le arrivava con la posta della sera. Stava leggendo delle persecuzioni religiose nel Messico, quando suonò il campanello. – Vittoria, – chiamò la signorina. Vittoria stava rigovernando e siccome era un po' sorda non sentí. Con un'espressione sofferente, la signorina andò lei ad aprire. Era la lattaia. La signorina accentuò l'espressione sofferente.

La lattaia si scusò di essere venuta a quell'ora, ma disse, durante il giorno era sempre occupata col negozio ... – Un minuto solo, signorina –. La signorina la fece passare nel salottino, ma non le disse di sedere. – Venivo per quel mio cognato, – riprese la donna. – Lei sa, quello che è infermiere all'ospedale ... – La signorina disse che ricordava benissimo. Era stata lei stessa ad adoperarsi perché fosse assunto.

Si trattava di questo: ora che il capo infermiere aveva raggiunto i limiti di età, si sarebbe liberato un posto nell'organico: era l'occasione propizia per far entrare in pianta stabile il cognato. C'era un altro aspirante, che aveva meno anzianità e che inoltre era scapolo. Ma, a quanto risultava a suo cognato, aveva l'appoggio del Fascio...[6]

– Capisce, signorina: se mio cognato potesse entrare in pianta stabile, sarebbe tutta un'altra cosa. Intanto, la paga verrebbe a essergli quasi raddoppiata, e poi avrebbe la sicurezza per l'avvenire ... Perché un avventizio può essere sempre mandato via da un momento all'altro. Basta che cambi il direttore ... – Non soltanto il cognato aveva diritto perché piú anziano e per il carico di famiglia; ma era anche un lavoratore, che all'ospedale si era fatto benvolere, tanto dai malati che dalle suore ... – Non chiediamo mica[7] un favoritismo, signorina; chiediamo il giusto. Provi a domandarlo alle suore, se sono contente di lui ...

– È vero che maltratta la moglie? – disse improvvisamente la signorina. – Mi hanno detto anche che la picchia.

meal, she unwrapped the *Osservatore Romano*, which arrived by the evening post. She was reading about the religious persecution in Mexico when the bell rang. 'Vittoria!' she cried. Vittoria, who was washing up, was a little deaf and did not hear. With a suffering expression on her face, the signorina went to open the door herself. It was the milk-woman. The signorina's expression of suffering increased.

The milk-woman apologized for having come at this hour of the day, but said that during the day-time she was always busy in the shop. 'Just one minute, signorina!' The signorina took her into the small drawing-room, but did not ask her to sit down. 'I've come on behalf of that brother-in-law of mine,' continued the woman. 'You know, the one who's an orderly at the hospital.' The signorina said she remembered him very well. It was she who had done her best to get him taken on there.

The problem now was that the head orderly had reached the retiring age, and his post on the staff had become vacant. It was just the moment for her brother-in-law to get a permanent job. There was another candidate, less senior and who was, moreover, a bachelor. But – in the opinion of her brother-in-law – this man had the support of the Fascio.

'You realize, signorina, that if my brother-in-law could have a sure job things would be very different. Then the pay would be nearly double, and it would offer security for the future.... Because a casual labourer can be dismissed at any moment. All that's needed is a change in management.' It was right that her brother-in-law should have the job, not only because he was an older man and had the responsibility of a family, but because he was a worker who had made himself liked at the hospital, as much by the patients as by the nuns. 'We certainly aren't asking a favour, signorina. We only want what is just. You've only to ask the sisters if they're pleased with him ...'

'Is it true that he ill-treats his wife?' said the signorina suddenly. 'I've heard he beats her, too!'

La lattaia rimase sconcertata; ma si riprese subito:

– In famiglia, questo è vero, non vanno tanto d'accordo. Ma, cosa crede? la colpa di tutto, è la miseria. Quando un uomo porta a casa centoventicinque lire[8] la quindicina, e con quelle deve pagare l'affitto, la luce, il carbone, e dar da mangiare a quattro bocche, lei capisce che i soldi non possono bastare. E allora, per forza, lui è di cattivo umore, la moglie lo stesso, e le occasioni dei litigi sono facili.

– Ma voi un po' d'aiuto glielo date.

– Qualcosa, certo, gli diamo, – disse la donna, – dopo tutto si tratta di mia sorella, dei bambini di mia sorella ... E mio marito, è il primo lui a dire: Aiutiamoli. Come se fossero parenti suoi ...

La signorina promise che ci avrebbe messo[9] una buona parola. – La porta, la trova da sé, – disse interrompendo i ringraziamenti della lattaia.

Passò di cucina a dir qualcosa alla donna, e si ritirò in camera.

La camera era piccola, imbiancata a calce; e a differenza delle altre stanze, era semplice e nuda. In camera la signorina aveva appunto voluto ispirarsi a una nudità francescana. La chiamava «la mia celletta». Dalla ringhiera del letto di ferro pendeva un ramo d'olivo; sopra il cassettone una stampa a colori raffigurava San Francesco nell'atto di ricevere le Stimmate.

La signorina si spogliò, si tolse lo scapolare,[10] infilò la camicia da notte, poi davanti allo specchio del cassettone sciolse i lunghi capelli ormai grigi. Quindi si coricò e spense la luce.

Mentre le sue labbra mormoravano i Pater, gli Ave, i Gloria e i Requiem, e poi la preghiera speciale composta dal Papa per le Terziarie,[11] la sua mente era occupata altrove. Dal vicolo venivano voci e risate. Per l'appunto lí sotto c'era una bettola. Ancora voci, ancora risate, poi una sonora bestemmia.

The milk-woman looked disconcerted, but she continued immediately:

'It's true that they don't get on very well in the house. But what do you expect? Poverty, that's what's at the bottom of everything. When a man comes home once a fortnight with 125 lire and has to pay the rent with it, the electric light, the coal, and feed four mouths, you'll agree it's not enough. And then of course he gets into a temper. So does she, and it's easy to quarrel like that.'

'But you help them a bit?'

'Yes, of course we give them something,' said the woman. 'After all, it's my sister, and my sister's children. . . . And my husband, he's the first to say, Let's help them! – as if they were his own relations . . .'

The signorina promised she would put in a good word for them. 'You can find your own way to the door, can't you?' she said, interrupting the thanks of the milk-woman.

She went into the kitchen to have a word with the maid, and then into her bedroom.

It was a small room, whitewashed – unlike the others, simple and unadorned. Franciscan bareness was exactly what she had wanted as inspiration here; she called it 'my little cell'. From the iron bed rail hung an olive branch; above the chest of drawers a coloured print showed Saint Francis in the act of receiving the Stigmata.

The signorina undressed, took off her scapular, put on her night-dress and then, in front of the mirror on the chest of drawers, let down her long hair which was now grey. She then got into bed and put out the light.

While her lips murmured the Pater, the Ave Maria, the Gloria, and the Requiem, and the special prayer composed by the Pope for the Tertiaries, her mind was busy elsewhere. Voices and laughter came up from the alley immediately below, where there was a wine booth. More voices, more laughter – then a resounding oath.

I POVERI

«Sono proprio bestie», pensò la signorina. Si voltò su un fianco. Era ormai vicina ad addormentarsi, quando si ricordò che anche quel giorno aveva pensato male e sparlato della Ormanni. Si disse che doveva tenerlo a mente per la confessione.

'What beasts they are!' she thought, turning over onto her side. She was half asleep when she remembered that during the same day she had thought and spoken badly of the Ormanni woman. She must bear this in mind at Confession.

BIG FISH, LITTLE FISH
ITALO CALVINO

Translated by Archibald Colquhoun

PESCI GROSSI, PESCI PICCOLI

Il padre di Zeffirino non si metteva mai in costume da bagno. Stava in calzoni rimboccati e maglietta, con in capo il berretto di tela bianca, e non si staccava mai dalla scogliera. La sua passione erano le patelle, i piatti molluschi che stanno appiccicati allo scoglio, e fanno col loro durissimo guscio quasi tutt'uno con la pietra. Per staccarle il padre di Zeffirino adoperava un coltello, e ogni domenica col suo sguardo occhialuto passava in rassegna una per una le rocce della punta. Continuava finché la sua piccola cesta non era piena di patelle; qualcuna la mangiava appena colta, succhiandone la polpa umida ed agra come da un cucchiaio; le altre le metteva in una cesta. Ogni tanto alzava gli occhi, li girava un po' spersi sul mare liscio e chiamava: – Zeffirino! Dove sei?

Zeffirino passava in acqua pomeriggi interi. Venivano alla punta tutti e due, e il padre lo lasciava lí e subito si metteva dietro ai suoi molluschi. Cosí ferme e testarde, le patelle non potevano attirare Zeffirino; furono dapprima i granchi, a interessarlo, poi i polpi, le meduse, e poi via via tutte le qualità di pesci. D'estate le sue cacce erano sempre piú difficili e ingegnose: e adesso non c'era ragazzetto della sua età che col fucile subacqueo andasse cosí bene come lui. In acqua chi va meglio sono i tipi un po' tracagnotti, tutti fiato e muscolo; e Zeffirino veniva su cosí. Visto a terra, per mano a suo padre, era uno di quei ragazzi rapati e a bocca aperta da far andare avanti a scappellotti; invece in acqua dava punti a tutti;[1] sott'acqua meglio ancora.

Quel giorno Zeffirino era riuscito a mettere insieme tutto l'armamento per la caccia subacquea. La maschera l'aveva già dall'anno scorso, regalo di sua nonna; una

BIG FISH, LITTLE FISH

Zeffirino's father never got into bathing-dress. He stayed in rolled-up trousers and vest, with a white linen cap on his head, and never moved away from the rocks. He had a passion for limpets, the flat clams which stick to rocks and become with their very hard shells almost part of the stone. To prise them off Zeffirino's father used a knife, and every Sunday he would scrutinize the rocks on the headland one by one through his spectacled eyes. On he would go until his little basket was full of limpets; some he ate as soon as gathered, sucking the damp bitter pulp as if from a spoon; the rest he put into his basket. Every now and again he would raise his eyes, let them meander over the smooth sea and call out: 'Zeffirino! Where are you?'

Zeffirino spent whole afternoons in the water. They would go together as far as the point, then his father left him there and went straight off after his clams. Limpets were no attraction to Zeffirino, they were so motionless and stubborn; what interested him most were crabs, then octopuses, jelly-fish, and then eventually any kind of fish. In summer his hunts became ever more arduous and resourceful; and now there was not a boy of his age who was so good with an underwater gun as he. In water the types that go best are rather stocky, all lungs and muscle; and Zeffirino was growing up like that. Seen on land, holding his father's hand, he was one of those crop-haired, open-mouthed boys who need clouting to drive along; but in water he outdid everyone; underwater better still.

That day Zeffirino had managed to put together a complete gear for underwater fishing. The mask he already had from the year before, a present from his grandmother; a

71

cugina che aveva i piedi piccoli gli prestò le pinne; il fucile lo prese a casa di suo zio senza dir niente e al padre disse che gliel'avevano prestato. D'altronde era un bambino attento, che sapeva usare e tener di conto tutto, e ci si poteva fidare a dargli roba in prestito. [1a]

Il mare era una bellezza, cosí limpido. Zeffirino disse: Sí, papà, – a tutte le raccomandazioni e andò in acqua. Con quel muso di vetro e l'antenna per respirare, le gambe che finivano da pesce, e in mano quell'arnese[2] un po' lancia un po' fucile e un po' forchetta, non somigliava piú a un essere umano. Invece, appena in mare, benché filasse via mezzo sommerso, subito si riconosceva che era lui: dal colpo che dava con le pinne, dal modo in cui il fucile gli sporgeva sottobraccio, dall'impegno che metteva ad andare avanti con la testa giú a fior d'acqua.

Il fondo dapprincipio era di sassi, poi di rocce, alcune nude e corrose, altre barbute di fitte alghe brune. Da ogni piega di scoglio, o tra le tremule barbe librate alla corrente, poteva a un tratto apparire un grosso pesce; dietro il vetro della maschera Zeffirino muoveva attento intorno gli occhi ansiosi.

Un fondo marino è bello la prima volta, quando lo si scopre: ma il piú bello, come in ogni cosa, viene dopo, a impararlo tutto, bracciata per bracciata. Pare di berli, i paesaggi acquatici: si va si va e non si finirebbe mai. Il vetro della maschera è un enorme unico occhio per ingoiare le ombre e i colori. Ora lo scuro finiva e s'era fuori da quel mar di scoglio;[3] sulla sabbia del fondo si distinguevano le sottili crespe disegnate dal muoversi del mare. I raggi del sole arrivavano fin giú con luminelli occhieggianti e luccichii di branchi di rincorri-gli-ami:[4] minutissimi pescetti che filano dritti dritti e a un tratto svoltano ad angolo retto tutti insieme.

Si levò una piccola nuvola di sabbia ed era il colpo di coda di un sarago sul fondo. Non s'era accorto d'avere puntata contro quella fiocina. Zeffirino già nuotava immerso; e il sarago, dopo poche mosse distratte dei fianchi striati, di soprassalto filò via a mezz'acqua[5]. Tra scogli

girl cousin with small feet lent him the flippers; the gun he had taken from his uncle's home without saying anything and told his father they had lent it. Anyway he was a careful little boy, who knew how to use and take care of everything and could be trusted with a loan of them.

The sea was lovely, so clear. Zeffirino said 'Yes, dad' to all his father's advice and went into the water. With that glass snout and that breathing tube, his legs ending like a fish's, his hands gripping that weapon, part spear, part gun, and part fork, he no longer looked like a human being. But as soon as he was in the sea, though he slipped along half-submerged, one could see it was him at once; from the shove he gave with his flippers, the way his gun jutted under his arm, the care he took to move along with head down on the surface of the water.

At first the sea-bed was of pebbles, then of rocks, some bare and corroded, others bearded with thick brown seaweed. From every fold of rock, or between the quivering beards of weed poised in the current, there might suddenly appear a big fish; behind the glass of his mask Zeffirino moved around anxious attentive eyes.

A sea-bed is lovely the first time when one discovers it; but it's lovelier afterwards like everything else, when one gets to learn all about it, stroke by stroke. One seems to be drinking them, these marine landscapes; on and on, one goes and might go on for ever. The glass of the mask is a huge single eye to swallow up shadows and colours. Now the dark ended and he was out of that boulder-strewn part; on the sand of the bottom could be made out fine crinkles drawn by the movement of the sea. The sun's rays reached right down with peering gleams amid twinkling shoals of tiny fish swimming along in a straight line then suddenly all turning together at a right angle.

A little cloud of sand went up from the blow of a sea-bream's tail on the bottom. It had not noticed that harpoon pointing at it. Zeffirino was now swimming right under water; and the bream, after a few distracted movements of its striped sides, all of a sudden rushed away closer to the

irti di ricci il pesce e il pescatore nuotarono fino a una cala di roccia porosa e quasi nuda. «Qui non mi scappa», pensò Zeffirino; e in quel momento il sarago sparí. Da buchi e incavi si levava un filo di bollicine d'aria, poi subito smetteva e riprendeva altrove; gli anemoni marini brillavano in attesa. Il sarago fece capolino da una tana,[6] sparí in un'altra e sbucò subito da un pertugio distantissimo. Bordeggiò uno sperone di roccia, puntò in basso e Zeffirino vide verso il fondo una zona d'un verde luminoso. Il pesce si perdette in quella luce, e Zeffirino gli andò dietro.

Traversò un basso arco al piede della roccia e riebbe sopra di sé l'acqua alta e il cielo. Ombre di pietra chiara circondavano il fondo tutt'intorno e verso il largo s'abbassavano in una scogliera mezzo sommersa. Con un colpo di reni ed una spinta delle pinne Zeffirino riemerse a respirare. Il tubo dell'aria affiorò, soffiò via qualche goccia infiltrata nella maschera, ma la testa del ragazzo restò in acqua. Aveva ritrovato il sarago; anzi: due! Già lui mirava quando ne vide tutta una squadra[7] navigare tranquilla alla sinistra, ed a destra brillare un altro branco. Era un posto ricchissimo di pesca, quasi uno specchio chiuso, e dovunque Zeffirino guardasse incontrava un guizzare di pinne sottili, luccichii di squame, tanto che dallo stupore e dalla gioia non gli venne di far partire neanche un colpo.

Bisognava non aver fretta e studiare le botte migliori senza seminare intorno lo spavento. Zeffirino sempre a testa sotto si diresse verso lo scoglio piú vicino; e nella acqua, lungo la parete, vide una bianca mano penzolante. Il mare era immobile; sulla superficie tesa e tersa s'allargavano circoli concentrici come a un gocciolio di pioggia. Il ragazzo alzò il capo e guardò. Bocconi sull'orlo dello scoglio, una donna grassa in costume da bagno stava prendendo il sole. E piangeva. Le lagrime scendevano una dopo l'altra per le guance e cadevano nel mare.

surface. Fish and fisherman went swimming off between rocks bristling with sea-urchins until they reached a cove of porous, almost bare rock. 'Here it won't give me the slip,' thought Zeffirino; and at that moment the bream vanished. From holes and cavities rose a row of air bubbles which quickly stopped and started again elsewhere; sea-anemones gleamed in expectation. The bream peeped out of one hole, vanished into another and reappeared again at once from a distant aperture. It tacked along a spur of rock, headed down and Zeffirino saw a patch of luminous green towards the sea-bed. The fish lost itself in that light, and Zeffirino went after it.

He crossed a low arch at the foot of the rock and again had above him high sea and sky. Shadows of clear stone surrounded the sea-bed all round lowering into a half-submerged rock towards the open sea. With a thrust of his loins and a shove at his flippers Zeffirino re-emerged to breathe. The air-tube surfaced, away blew some drops filtered into the mask; but the boy's head stayed in the water. He had found the sea-bream again; in fact two! Just as he was aiming he saw a whole squadron of them navigating calmly to the left, and another shoal gleaming to his right. The place was swarming with fish, almost an enclosed lake, and wherever Zeffirino looked he met a frisking of narrow fins and a gleaming of scales. Between amazement and delight he did not let off a single shot.

He must not hurry, must calculate the best shots without sowing terror around. Zeffirino, still with head under water, moved towards the nearest rock; and in the water, along the wall, he saw a white hand dangling. The sea was motionless; concentric circles were widening as if from a drop of rain on the tense, terse surface. The boy raised his head and looked. Face downwards on the edge of the rock was a fat woman in a bathing-dress taking the sun. And crying. The drops came down her cheeks one after the other and fell into the sea.

Zeffirino alzò la maschera sulla fronte e disse: – Scusi.

La donna grassa disse: – Figurati,⁸ ragazzo – e continuava a piangere. – Pesca pure.

– È un posto pieno di pesci – spiegò lui – Ha visto quanti?

La donna grassa restava col viso sollevato, gli occhi fissi davanti a sé pieni di lagrime – Non ho visto proprio. Come faccio? Non riesco a smettere di piangere.

Zeffirino finché si trattava di mare e di pesci era il piú in gamba;⁹ invece, in presenza di persone, riprendeva quella sua aria a bocca aperta e balbuziente – Mi dispiace, signora ... – e avrebbe voluto tornarsene ai suoi saraghi, ma una donna grassa piangente era una vista cosí insolita che lui restava incantato a guardarla suo malgrado.

– Non sono signora, ragazzo, – disse la donna grassa con quella sua voce nobile e un po' nasale. – Chiamami signorina. Signorina De Magistris. E tu come ti chiami?

– Zeffirino.

– Bravo, Zeffirino. Hai fatto buona pesca? O buona caccia, come si dice?

– Non so come si dica. Non ho ancora preso niente. Qui però è un buon posto.

– Sta' attento con quel fucile, però. Non per me, poveretta me. Ma per te, a non farti male.

Zeffirino la assicurò che poteva star tranquilla. Si sedette sullo scoglio accanto a lei e la guardò un po' piangere. C'erano momenti in cui sembrava che smettesse, e allora aspirava dal naso arrossato, alzando e scotendo il capo. Ma intanto agli angoli degli occhi e sotto le palpebre era come si gonfiasse una bolla di lagrime e l'occhio subito ne traboccava.

Zeffirino non sapeva bene che pensare. Vedere una signorina che piangeva era una cosa che stringeva il cuore. Ma come si faceva ad essere tristi davanti a quel recinto marino colmo di tutte le varietà di pesci, che riempiva il cuore di gioia e di voglia? E a tuffarsi in

Zeffirino raised his mask onto his forehead and said 'Excuse me.'

The fat woman said, 'Of course, boy,' and went on crying. 'Do please go on fishing.'

'It's full of fish, this place is,' he explained. 'Have you seen how many there are?'

The fat woman lay with face raised, her eyes staring ahead full of tears. 'I haven't really looked. How can I? I just can't manage to stop crying.'

Zeffirino was at his best in matters of sea and fishes; but in the presence of people he took on that stuttering open-mouthed air of his again.

'I'm sorry, signora . . .' and he would have turned back to his breams; but a fat woman crying was such an unusual sight that he stayed there spellbound, gazing at her in spite of himself.

'I'm not a signora, boy,' said the fat woman in that noble rather nasal voice of hers. 'Call me Signorina. Signorina De Magistris. And what's your name?'

'Zeffirino.'

'Fine, Zeffirino. Have you had a good fish? Or a good hunt? What do they call it?'

'I don't know what they call it. I haven't caught anything yet. But this is a good place here.'

'Be careful with that gun, though. Not for my sake, poor little me. But for your own, not to hurt yourself.'

Zeffirino assured her that she need not worry. He sat down on the rock next to her and watched her crying for a bit. There were moments in which she seemed to be stopping; then she would breathe through her reddened nose, raising and shaking her head. But meanwhile in the corners of her eyes and under her lids a bubble of tears seemed to be swelling up and her eye quickly overflowed.

Zeffirino didn't know quite what to think. To see a signorina crying like that wrung his heart. But how could one be sad facing that marine pen brim-full of every variety of fish, and filling his heart with joy and longing? As to plunging into that green water and going after the fish, how

quel verde e ad andare dietro ai pesci, come si faceva
con vicino una persona grande tutta in lagrime? Nello
stesso momento, nello stesso posto esistevano insieme due
struggimenti[10] cosí opposti e inconciliabili. Zeffirino non
riusciva a pensarli entrambi insieme; né a lasciarsi andare
all'uno o all'altro.

– Signorina, – chiese.
– Dimmi.
– Perché piange?
– Perché sono sfortunata in amore.
– Ah!
– Tu non puoi capire, sei un ragazzo.
– Vuol provare a nuotare con la maschera?
– Grazie, volentieri. È bello?
– È la cosa piú bella che ci sia.

La signorina De Magistris si alzò e s'abbottonò le
bretelline del costume sulla schiena. Zeffirino le diede la
maschera e le spiegò bene come metterla. Lei mosse un
po' il capo tra scherzosa e vergognosa con la maschera
sul viso, ma in trasparenza si vedevano gli occhi che non
smettevano di piangere. Scese in mare senza grazia,
come una foca, e prese ad annaspare tenendo il viso giú.

Zeffirino col fucile sottobraccio si buttò a nuoto anche
lui.

– Quando vede un pesce m'avverta, – gridò alla De
Magistris. In acqua lui non scherzava; e il privilegio di
venire a pescare con lui lo concedeva raramente.

Ma la signorina alzava il capo e faceva segno di no. Il
vetro era diventato opaco e non si vedevano piú i tratti
del suo viso. Si tolse la maschera. – Non vedo niente, –
disse, – le lagrime mi appannano il vetro. Non posso.
Mi dispiace –. E restava lí, piangente, in acqua.

– È un guaio, – disse Zeffirino. Non aveva con sé la
mezza patata da sfregare sul vetro per farlo ritornare
limpido, ma s'arrangiò alla meglio con un po' di saliva e
indossò lui la maschera. – Guardi come faccio io, – disse
alla grassa. E avanzarono insieme per quel mare, lui
tutto di pinne con la testa giú, lei nuotando su un fianco,

could one do that with a grown-up in tears nearby? At the same moment, at the same place, coexisted two opposite, irreconcilable urges. Zeffirino could not manage to think of both together; nor of letting himself go to one or the other.

'Signorina,' he asked.
'Yes?'
'Why are you crying?'
'Because I'm crossed in love.'
'Ah!'
'You can't understand, you're only a boy.'
'Would you like to try and swim with the mask?'
'Thank you, I'd love to. Is it nice?'
'It's the nicest thing ever.'
Signorina De Magistris got up and buttoned the straps of her bathing-dress on her back. Zeffirino gave her the mask and explained carefully how to put it on. She moved her head a little with the mask over her face, part-joking and part-coy, but through the glass could be seen her eyes which never stopped crying. She went into the sea grace-lessly, like a seal, and began to hold her face down gaspingly.

Zeffirino, gun under arm, jumped in and swam too.

'Tell me when you see a fish,' he called to Signorina De Magistris. In water he never joked; coming to fish with him was a privilege he rarely conceded.

But the signorina raised her head and shook it. The glass had gone opaque and her features were not to be seen any-more. She took off the mask. 'I can't see a thing,' she said, 'the tears are dulling the glass. I can't do it. Sorry.' And she remained there in the water, weeping.

'What a mess,' said Zeffirino. He had no half-potato with him to rub on the glass and make it come clear again, but did the best he could with a little saliva, then put on the mask himself. 'Watch how I do it,' he said to the fat woman. And they moved on together over that sea, he all flippers with his head down, she swimming sidestroke, with one

79

con un braccio disteso e l'altro piegato, e il capo amaramente eretto e inconsolabile.

Nuotava male, la signorina De Magistris, tutto di fianco, con un goffo slancio di bracciate. E sotto di lei per metri e metri i pesci correvano il mare, navigavano stelle marine e seppie, s'aprivano le bocche delle attinie. Ecco che allo sguardo di Zeffirino si facevano incontro paesaggi da lasciarcisi smarrire. L'acqua era alta e il fondo sabbioso era cosparso di piccoli scogli tra i quali dondolavano matasse d'alghe al moto appena sensibile del mare. Ma a guardare di lassú, sulla distesa uniforme della sabbia sembrava fossero gli scogli ad ondeggiare in mezzo all'acqua ferma e densa d'alghe.

A un tratto la De Magistris se lo vide sparire a testa in giú, affiorare un istante col sedere, poi con le pinne e poi la sua ombra chiara era sott'acqua, che calava verso il fondo. Fu troppo tardi quando il lupaccio s'accorse del pericolo: la fiocina scattata già l'aveva colto di sbieco e il dente di mezzo gli si conficcò verso la coda e lo passò da parte a parte. Il lupaccio drizzò le pinne spinose e s'avventò battendo l'acqua, gli altri denti della fiocina non l'avevano preso e lui sperava ancora di fuggire a costo di scodarsi. Ma quel che ci guadagnò fu di infiggersi una pinna su uno dei denti liberi, e fu perso. Il rocchetto ritirava già il filo e l'ombra rosea e contenta di Zeffirino gli era sopra.

La fiocina apparve fuori dall'acqua col lupaccio infilzato, poi il braccio del ragazzo, poi la testa mascherata e un gorgoglio d'acqua dalla canna. E Zeffirino si scoperse il viso: -- Visto che bello? Visto, signorina? – Era un grosso lupaccio argenteo e nero. Però la donna continuava a piangere.

Zeffirino si arrampicò sulla punta di uno scoglio; la De Magistris lo seguí a fatica. Per posare il pesce in fresco il ragazzo scelse una piccola conca piena d'acqua. E ci si accoccolarono vicino. Zeffirino contemplava i cangianti colori del lupaccio, carezzava le scaglie e voleva che la De Magistris lo imitasse.

arm out and the other folded, and her head bitterly erect and inconsolable.

She swam badly, did Signorina De Magistris, all on one side, with clumsy sweeping strokes. And beneath her for yards and yards fishes coursed the sea, star-fish and cuttle-fish navigated, the mouths of sea-anemones opened. Now Zeffirino's eyes met seascapes that were quite bewildering. The tide was high and the sandy bottom was scattered with little rocks among which swayed clumps of seaweed moving to the faint movement of the sea. But looked at from above on that uniform stretch of sand it was the rocks that seemed to be waving about amid the still water dense with seaweed.

Suddenly Signorina De Magistris saw him vanish with head down, surface a second with his behind, then with the flippers, and then his clear shadow was under water, swooping down towards the sea-bed. When the bass noticed the danger it was too late; the loosed harpoon had already hit it aslant and the middle prong was stuck near its tail, piercing right through. The bass straightened its spiky fins and rushed off beating the water, the other prongs of the harpoon had not hit it and it still hoped to escape at the cost of shedding its tail. But all it gained was to impale a fin on one of the free prongs, and it was lost. The reel was already pulling in its cord, and the pink, pleased shadow of Zeffirino was above.

The harpoon appeared out of the water with the bass skewered on it, then the boy's arm, then his masked head and a gurgle of water from the barrel. And Zeffirino uncovered his face. 'D'you see what a fine one? D'you see, signorina?' The bass was a big silvery black one. But the woman went on crying.

Zeffirino clambered on to the top of a rock; Signorina De Magistris followed with some difficulty. To keep the fish fresh the boy chose a little rock-pool full of water, and they crouched down by it. Zeffirino watched the changing colours of the bass, stroked its scales and wanted Signorina De Magistris to imitate him.

– Vede che bello? Vede come punge? – Quando gli
parve che un filo d'interessamento per il pesce si facesse
largo nello sconforto della donna grassa, disse: – Io vado
a vedere un momentino se ne piglio un altro, – e, bardato
di tutto punto, si tuffò.

La donna restò col pesce. E scoperse che non v'era mai
stato pesce piú infelice. Ora lei passava le dita sulla bocca
ad anello, sulle branchie, sulla coda; ecco vedeva aprirsi,
nel bel corpo d'argento, mille fori minutissimi. Pulci
acquatiche, minuscoli parassiti dei pesci, s'erano da tempo impadronite del lupaccio e rodevano le loro vie nella
sua carne.

Ignaro di queste cose, Zeffirino già riemergeva con
sulla forchetta un'ombrina dorata, e la porgeva alla
signorina De Magistris. Cosí già i due si erano divisi i
compiti: la donna toglieva il pesce dalla fiocina e lo metteva in fresco nella conca; e Zeffirino si ficcava di nuovo
a testa in acqua per cacciarne un altro. Ma prima guardava ogni volta se la De Magistris aveva smesso di piangere
se non smetteva a vedere un lupaccio, un'ombrina, cosa
mai avrebbe potuto consolarla?

Strie dorate traversavano i fianchi dell'ombrina. Due
pinne in fila percorrevano il suo dorso. E nell'intervallo
tra queste pinne, la signorina vide una ferita stretta e
profonda piú antica di quelle della fiocina. Un colpo di
becco di gabbiano doveva aver picchiato sul dorso del
pesce con tanta forza che non si capiva come non l'avesse
ucciso. Chissà da quando l'ombrina portava con sé
questo dolore.

Piú veloce della fiocina di Zeffirino, sopra un branco
di zerli[11] piccoli e incerti, s'abbatteva il dentice. Fece in
tempo a inghiottire uno zerlo e la forchetta gli s'inca-
strava in gola. Mai Zeffirino aveva fatto un colpo tanto
buono.

– Un dentice mondiale! – gridò, togliendosi la maschera. – Io ero dietro agli zerli! Ne inghiotte uno ed io ... –
e spiegava la scena esprimendo la commozione a balbettii.
Un pesce piú grosso e bello era impossibile cacciarlo: e

'D'you see what a fine one? D'you see how it pricks?'
When he thought that there was a faint interest in the fish
leavening the fat woman's misery, he said, 'I'll just try a
moment and see if I can catch another.' In full harness he
dived.

The woman stayed with the fish. And she discovered that
never had a fish been so unhappy. She began passing her
fingers on its ring-like mouth, its gills, its tail; and now all
over its lovely silvery body she saw thousands of tiny per-
forations. Water fleas, minute parasites of fish, had become
masters of the bass for some time and were gnawing their
way into its flesh.

Ignorant of all this, Zeffirino now re-emerged with a
sea-perch on his harpoon, and proffered it to Signorina De
Magistris. So the two had already divided tasks; she took
the fish from the harpoon and put it to keep cool in the
rock-pool; and Zeffirino again plunged in head-first to
catch another. Before he did so he looked every time to see
if Signorina De Magistris had stopped crying; if she did not
stop at sight of a bass or a sea-perch, what on earth could
ever console her?

Golden stripes went across the sides of the sea-perch. Two
rows of fins went up its back. And in the gap between these
fins the signorina saw a deep narrow wound that had been
there before the harpoon's. A seagull's beak must have
bitten into the fish's back so sharply that she could not
understand why it had not been killed. Who knows how
long the perch had taken this agony about with it?

Faster than Zeffirino's harpoon, a bream fell on a shoal
of little uncertain whitebait. It was just in time to swallow a
whitebait before the harpoon was embedded in its throat.
Never had Zeffirino made such a good shot.

'It's an outsize dentex!' he cried, taking off his mask.
'I was following the whitebait! It'd swallowed one and I
...' and he explained the scene, showing his excitement by
his stutter. No bigger or finer fish was possible to catch;

Zeffirino avrebbe voluto finalmente che la De Magistris prendesse parte alla sua soddisfazione. Lei guardava il grasso corpo argentato, quella gola che aveva or ora inghiottito il pesciolino verdastro a sua volta sbranata dai denti della fiocina: e cosí era la vita in tutto il mare.

Zeffirino pescò ancora un rocché[12] grigio e un rocché rosso, un sarago a strisce gialle, un'orata grassotta ed una piatta boga; perfino un baffuto e spinoso pescerondine. Ma in tutti, oltre alle ferite della fiocina, la signorina De Magistris scopriva la puntura della pulce che li aveva rosi, o la macchia d'una peste sconosciuta, o l'amo conficcato da tempo nella gola. Quella cala scoperta dal ragazzo, dove tutte le specie di pesci si davano convegno, era forse un rifugio d'animali condannati a una lunga agonia, un lazzaretto[13] marino, un'arena di duelli disperati.

Ora Zeffirino armeggiava tra gli scogli: i polpi! Ne aveva scoperto una colonia appiattata al piede di un masso. Sulla forchetta già affiorava un grosso polpo violaceo stillando dalle ferite un liquido simile ad inchiostro annacquato; ed una strana ansia s'impadroní della signorina De Magistris. Per contenere il polpo fu trovata una conca appartata e Zeffirino non si sarebbe piú mosso di lí, ad ammirare la pelle grigio-rosa che cambiava lentamente sfumature. Era anche tardi e al ragazzo cominciava a venire un po' di pelle d'oca, tanto era stato lungo quel suo bagno. Ma non era certo Zeffirino che rinunciava a una famiglia di polpi già scoperta.

La signorina osservava il polpo, la sua carne viscida, le bocche delle ventose, l'occhio rossiccio e quasi liquido. Ed ecco che il polpo, unico tra gli esseri pescati, a lei sembrava senza macchia né tormento. I tentacoli d'un roseo quasi umano, cosí molli e sinuosi, e pieni d'ascelle segrete, richiamavano pensieri di salute e vita, e ancora qualche torpida contrazione li faceva volgere con un lieve dilatare di ventose. La mano della signorina De Magistris accennava a mezz'aria una carezza sulle spire

and Zeffirino would have liked Signorina De Magistris to take part in his pleasure at last. She looked at the plump silvery body, that throat which had just a moment before swallowed the greenish little fish and been in its turn torn to shreds by the harpoon's teeth. Such was life in the entire sea.

Zeffirino fished out yet a grey rock-fish and a red rock-fish, a bream with yellow stripes, a fat dory and a flat bogue; even a hairy and prickly flying fish. But in each of them, apart from harpoon wounds, Signorina De Magistris found the pricks of fleas that had gnawed at them, or the mark of an unknown disease, or a fish-hook stuck in its gullet some time ago. That cove discovered by the boy, where every sort of fish met, was perhaps a refuge for creatures condemned to a long death agony, a marine hospital, an arena for desperate duels.

Zeffirino was now manoeuvring among the rocks. Octopuses! He had discovered a colony hidden at the foot of a boulder. The harpoon had already surfaced a big lilac octopus, its wounds dripping with liquid like watered ink; and a strange anguish now came over Signorina De Magistris. To hold the octopus a separate rock-pool was found and Zeffirino felt like staying there for ever, lost in admiration of the grey-pink skin slowly changing colour. It was also late and the boy was beginning to get a little goose-flesh, his bathe had been so long. But Zeffirino was certainly not one to renounce a family of octopuses already discovered.

The signorina was examining the octopus, its slimy flesh, the mouths of the suckers, the reddish almost liquid eye. And the octopus seemed to her the only one among the creatures fished up to be without a mark or sign of torment. Its tentacles of almost human pink, so soft and sinuous and full of secret suckers, made her think of health and life; some torpid contraction was still making them turn with a slight dilation of the suckers. Signorina De Magistris's hand sketched a caress above the coils of the octopus and she

del polpo e muoveva le dita imitandone il contrarsi, e poi sempre piú avvicinandosi arrivò a sfiorarle.

Scendeva la sera, un'onda incominciava a battere sul mare. I tentacoli vibrarono in aria come fruste e subito il polpo era avvinghiato con tutta la sua forza al braccio della signorina De Magistris. In piedi sullo scoglio, come fuggendo dal suo stesso braccio prigioniero, lanciò un grido che suonò come: – È il polpo! È il polpo che mi strazia!

Zeffirino, che era proprio allora riuscito a stanare un calamaro, mise il capo fuori dell'acqua e vide la donna grassa con il polpo che dal braccio allungava un tentacolo e la prendeva per la gola. Sentí la fine del grido, anche: era un urlo alto e continuo, ma – cosí parve al ragazzo – senza lagrime.

Accorse un uomo armato di un coltello e prese a sferrare colpi contro l'occhio del mollusco: lo decapitò quasi di netto. Era il padre di Zeffirino che riempita la sua cestina di patelle veniva a cercare il figlio per gli scogli. Udito l'urlo, appuntando il suo sguardo occhialuto aveva visto la donna ed era corso con la lama che usava per le patelle a darle aiuto. I tentacoli si afflosciarono subito; la signorina De Magistris svenne.

Quando ritornò in sé trovò il polpo tagliato a pezzi e Zeffirino e il padre glielo regalarono per cucinarlo fritto. Era sera e Zeffirino si era messo la maglietta. Il padre con gesti precisi le spiegò come si faceva un buon fritto di polpo. Zeffirino la guardava e diverse volte credette che fosse lí lí per ricominciare; invece, non le uscí piú neanche una lagrima.

moved her fingers imitating its contractions, getting closer and closer until she grazed it.

Evening was coming down, a wave beginning to beat in the sea. The tentacles vibrated in the air like whips, and suddenly the octopus was clinging tight with all its strength to Signorina De Magistris's arm. Standing on the rock as if trying to escape from her own imprisoned arm, she let out a cry which sounded like, 'The octopus! He's tearing me to bits!'

Zeffirino, who had just that second managed to dislodge a cuttlefish, put his head out of the water and saw the fat woman with one of the octupus's tentacles reaching from her arm to take her by the throat. He heard the end of her cry too; it was a high and continuous howl but – so the boy thought – without a sob.

Up rushed a man armed with a knife and began slashing blows down on the octopus's eye; he cut off its head almost clean. It was Zeffirino's father, who had filled his basket with clams and was coming along the rocks to look for his son. Hearing the shout, and adjusting his spectacles, he had seen the woman and rushed to her help with the knife he used for clams. The tentacles went flabby at once; Signorina De Magistris swooned.

When she came to herself she found the octopus cut in pieces: Zeffirino and his father gave it to her to fry. It was evening and Zeffirino had put on his vest. The father explained with precise gestures how to make a good fry-up of octopus. Zeffirino looked at her and a number of times thought she was on the very point of starting again; but no, not even one tear came out.

THE ASH OF BATTLES PAST
CARLO EMILIO GADDA

Translated by I. M. Rawson

LA CENERE DELLE BATTAGLIE

Eucarpio Vanzaghi, uomo probo e serio, dirigeva un'industria. Non era commendatore.[1] Godeva fama di psicologo, cioè di saper leggere nel cuore della gente, uomini e donne, grandi e piccini: arii e urofinnici.[2] Il suo lavoro lo «assorbiva»; non tuttavia fino a impedirgli, quando dava il caso, di adoperarsi per gli altri. Dacché acume psicologico e la sicurezza del giudizio, in Eucarpio, si accompagnavano alla bontà. Aveva cinquantacinque anni, un orologio d'oro da polso. Gli affari, spesso, lo mettevano in treno: allora, più che mai, consultava l'orologio. Aveva studiato, lavorato, perseverato: «lottava», come si suol dire: per sé, per i figli. Aveva moglie, tre figli: molto ben piantati, molto ben cresciuti. In casa, oltre le consuete provvidenze, c'era telefono e radio: acqua calda, tappeti. Tappetoni di Monza.[3] La famiglia e il lavoro gli avevano procurato le «soddisfazioni» più alte, la sana gioia del vivere. Qualche frattura di gamba dell'uno o dell'altro figlio skiante, o qualche migliaio di lirette[4] per le ripetizioni di matematica, non lo avevano eccessivamente inquietato. Poteva, poteva. Convinto fautore delle moderne cautele profilattiche, aveva offerto l'operazione dell'appendicite, oltreché a se stesso, a tutte le sorelle: come regalo di Natale: alle sorelle nel 1936, '37, '38: alla Giovanna, alla Emma, alla Teresa. La cosa era parecchio di moda nel 1920, ma le persone di giudizio tengono dietro alla moda con una certa ponderatezza: e nel frattempo, magari, la moda ha soffiato sulla sua girandola. Il fatto è che lo Zacchi, il chirurgo, aveva asportato alle tre signore tre magnifiche appendici. Alla clinica Biscaretti s'erano congratulati tutti, con ognuna

THE ASH OF BATTLES PAST

Eucarpio Vanzaghi, an upright and serious-minded man, was the manager of a factory. He was not a *commendatore*. He enjoyed a reputation as a psychologist, that is, of knowing how to see into people's hearts: the hearts of men and women, old and young, Aryan and Ugro-Finnic. His work 'absorbed' him; yet not in such a degree as to prevent him, when occasion arose, from exerting himself for others. For in Eucarpio, psychological insight and sureness of judgement were accompanied by good-heartedness. He was fifty-five years old, and wore a gold wrist-watch. His business often led him to travel by train: then, he would consult his watch more than ever. He had studied, worked hard, persevered: had 'battled', as it is customary to say, for himself, for his children. He had a wife, and three sons: well set-up, well grown. At home, besides the usual services, there were the telephone and the wireless; hot water, carpets. Big rugs from Monza. His family and his work had brought him the greatest of 'satisfactions', a healthy joy in living. He had never been unduly worried if one or other of his sons had broken a leg in ski-ing, or had cost him some few thousands of *lire* for coaching in mathematics. He could afford it. A convinced supporter of modern prophylactic precautions, he had, besides having his own appendix removed, offered the operation to all his sisters: as a Christmas present: in 1936, 1937 and 1938: to his sisters Emma, Giovanna and Teresa. The thing had been very much the mode in 1920, but sensible people follow the fashion with a certain deliberation: and in the meantime it may well be that it has changed, like a weathercock. The fact remains that Zacchi, the surgeon, had removed three magnificent appendices from the three ladies. At the Biscaretti Clinic everyone had congratulated each of the

delle tre degenti, per la bellezza e la rosea freschezza dell'ablata appendice (un mignoletto lungo tanto) e per la rapidità della cicatrizzazione. Eran gente sana, i Vanzaghi: del nostro vecchio ceppo, e del meglio. Lo Zacchi si era congratulato con sé stesso. La moglie di Eucarpio, signora Giuseppina, aveva rifiutato il regalo:

«Fattela aprir tu, la tua panciaccia: io non ne sento per nulla il bisogno.»

Viveva, Eucarpio, in una città industre, dove lo spettacolo della operosità comune è lieto incitamento a operare, e conforto a vivere. Quali erano le persone più vicine al suo cuore, dopo la moglie e i figlioli? Erano le sorelle, i cognati, i cugini, le cugine, i nipoti, gli abiatici[5] e i parenti tutti: le mogli dei cugini e i mariti delle cugine. L'ingegner Bottoni, vecchio furbo e sorridente dalla bazza di befana,[6] avendo sposato in seconde nozze una terza e molto matura cugina di Eucarpio, era subito entrato nell'ambito degli amatissimi. Per gli ex-compagni di scuola, poi, Eucarpio aveva una specie di culto. Gli ricordavano, chissà! gli anni giovani, quando tutto il mondo, per il suo chicchirichí di galletto, era un'alba infinita: gli riconducevano, con qualche grana[7] di più, la Bellezza[8] e la Felicità di quegli anni che le ragazze si volgevano, a guardarlo a filar via ritto ritto: e il suo colletto di smart diciassettenne era quasi altrettanto rigido, altrettanto conico e turrito del colletto del Poeta:[9] l'arbitro, allora, di ogni inamidata eleganza.

Eucarpio ignorava il mortificante cinismo che ci abbandona alla solitudine del cuore e ci condurrà disperati alla morte. Ignorava, perché li voleva ignorare, certi stanchi motti, o proverbi, come chi dica: parenti serpenti, amici nemici.[10] Fedele agli amici, fratello ai cugini, innamorato delle zie, entusiasta delle sue sorelle, la Giovanna, la Emma, la Teresa, avrebbe fatto, per i compagni di scuola, altrettanti pezzi del cuore:[11] uno per ogni ex-compagno, o compagna, di scuola.

three patients on the beauty and rosy freshness of the extracted appendix (the length of a little finger) and on the rapid healing of the scar. Healthy people, the Vanzaghi family: of our old stock, and the best. Zacchi had been pleased with himself. Eucarpio's wife, the Signora Giuseppina, had refused the present:

'You can have your own fat belly cut open: I don't feel any need for that sort of thing.'

Eucarpio lived in a busy town where the spectacle of common industry is a happy stimulus to work, and a consolation in living. Who were those persons nearest his heart, after his wife and children? They were his sisters, his in-laws, his cousins of both sexes, his nephews and nieces, all the descendants of his great-grandparents and every one of his relatives: with the wives and husbands of his cousins. Bottoni, a crafty and smiling old engineer with the protruding chin of a Befana, who had married as his second wife a very mature third cousin of Eucarpio's, immediately joined the circle of those most warmly loved. And then, for his ex-schoolfellows, Eucarpio had a kind of cult. They recalled – who knows? – the years of his youth, when the whole world was as an unending dawn to the cheerful crowing of this young cock: they brought back to him, together with some additional vexations, the Glory and Happiness of those years when the girls turned to look at him as he passed by, holding himself erect: a smart seventeen-year-old with a collar almost as stiff, almost as pointed and towering as that of the Poet who was then the arbiter of all starched elegance.

Eucarpio knew nothing of the mortifying cynicism that abandons us to loneliness of heart and leads us, in despair, to death. He ignored, because he wanted to ignore them, certain well-worn sayings, or proverbs, such as: sharper than the serpent's tooth, etc., and, best friends best enemies. Faithful to his friends, a brother to his cousins, in love with his aunts, an enthusiastic admirer of his sisters, Giovanna, Emma, and Teresa, he would have done anything in the world for his school-friends: the former companions, of both sexes, of his school-days.

Quest'amore, questo culto, è da riconnettersi al culto-base che uno ha di se stesso: e, dunque, alla struttura indelebile dell'io, dell'io affettivo: per cui ci sentiamo radicati alla ceppaia, santamente avvinti alla madre comune, la città, la gente, la casata, la patria, l'adorabile campanile[12] di Cormano due metri più lungo di quello di Brusuglio: gocce, coi nostri compagni di scuola e coi cugini, e perfino coi cognati, d'un sangue uno e medesimo. Un motivato se pure inconscio orgoglio, il cosiddetto rispetto di noi stessi, che è l'amido che ci manda pel mondo a collo ritto, rendeva inaccettabile, nonché impensabile, ad Eucarpio Vanzaghi, un giudizio negativo sui suoi cugini, o comunque limitativo dei loro meriti, certamente grandi, certamente rari: (basti dire che erano delle persone oneste). Antiorbaciano[13] per la pelle, pronunciava reverente, enfatizzandolo in una scansione liturgica, il nome di zia Maddalena, la signora Schioppi, morta di un cancro baciando il ritratto di Quel Tale.[24] Eucarpio non condivideva affatto le isteriche opinioni della defunta nei riguardi di Quel Tale: anzi le aborriva. Ma la defunta, non dovete dimenticarlo, era sua zia: madre di una nidiata di cugini.

Nella deferenza tenace di che perseguiva la di lei memoria, figurò dunque tutto un assortimento di affetti, e dei più degni d'encomio: in primis il culto dei morti, sì, dei defunti: deinde la dedizione alla famiglia, ove s'intenda, per famiglia, un mezzo magliaio[15] di persone: in terzo luogo la carità cristiana, il parce sepulto, o sepultae:[16] in quarto luogo lo spirito cavalleresco, dato che chi baciava quel tal ritratto era (non c'è bisogno di insistervi) una donna, e per di più malata, e di un male inesorabile: un carcinoma! In qual parte le avesse preso, poi, sarebbe indiscreto il mandare per le stampe. Questi nobili affetti potenziavano collegialmente il ricordo di zia Maddalena, come i fili d'acqua che escono dalla rosa d'un inaffiatoio inaffiano collegialmente un fil d'erba, per quanto secco.

This warm affection, this cult, is to be linked with the basic cult that each one of us has of himself: and, therefore, with the enduring structure of the ego, the emotional ego: through which we feel rooted in our own stock, bound by sacred bonds to our common mother, our city, people, kindred, fatherland, to the charming bell-tower of Cormano which is two metres higher than that of Brusuglio: all, with our school-fellows and cousins, even our in-laws, drops of one and the same blood. A well-justified if indeed unconscious pride, that so-called self-respect which is the stiffening that sends us about the world with head erect, rendered not only inacceptable but unthinkable to Eucarpio Vanzaghi a negative judgement upon his cousins or one in any way making reservations as to their merits: which were certainly great, certainly rare: (let it suffice to say that they were honest people). A dyed-in-the-wool anti-Fascist, he would pronounce in reverent tones and with a liturgical emphasis the name of his Aunt Maddalena, the Signora Schioppi, who had died of cancer kissing the portrait of That Man. Eucarpio did not at all share the hysterical opinions of the dead woman concerning That Man: indeed, he abhorred them. But, it must not be forgotten, she was his aunt: the mother of a brood of cousins.

In the persistent deference with which he continued to hold her memory, therefore, a whole assortment of feelings figured, and of a most praiseworthy kind: firstly, the cult of the dead, yes, of those who have done with life: next came family devotion, 'family' being understood in the sense of some hundreds of persons: in the third place, Christian charity, the *parce sepulto*, or *sepultae*: fourthly, the spirit of chivalry, given that the person who kissed a picture of that sort was (needless to say) a woman, and moreover a woman ill of a relentless malady: a carcinoma! In what part of her body she had been attacked it would, furthermore, be indiscreet to indicate in print. These noble feelings, in combination, kept the memory of Aunt Maddalena potent, as the fine threads of water issuing from the rose of a watering-can combine in sprinkling a blade of grass, however dry.

LA CENERE DELLE BATTAGLIE

Tra gli ex-compagni di scuola, tra i dilettissimi, c'era Prosdocimo: al quale Eucarpio si sentiva legato da una fraterna amicizia. Ma la vita di Prosdocimo, con la seconda guerra mondiale, o forse anche innanzi, aveva preso una cattiva piega. Anzitutto ... era andato a stare in un'altra città molto meno industre di quella su dove tutt'e due avevano declinato rose[17] al ginnasio. Aveva lasciato un impiego redditizio, e molto serio, per occuparsi di quisquilie. Si era ammalato di stomaco: aveva rinunciato a prender moglie: e viveva solo, come narrano che ami vivere il gufo: (e non è vero, prende moglie anche il gufo). Abitava quel che lui diceva una misera soffitta: un magnifico sopralzo, in realtà, costruito dal padron di casa in persona, ch'era ingegnere di gran merito, tant'è vero che era generale del genio. Nella soffitta ci pioveva, ma questo non c'entra. Prosdocimo godeva la disistima dei vicini: se una serva cantava, a mattina, se uggiolava un cane alla luna, da un orto abbandonato, gli prendevano le peggiori bizze. E poi non aveva più un soldo. E poi era pazzo. Su questo punto, Eucarpio, uomo di grande perspicacia quale s'è detto, non aveva ormai alcun dubbio. Comunque, nella sua altrettanto grande bontà, non aveva esitato ad offrire qualche aiuto all'amico, da fronteggiar la magra e la durezza degli anni, dopo la pioggia delle bombe, in attesa della «ricostruzione immancabile».[18]

Prosdocimo, inopinatamente, aveva accettato le sovvenzioni, cioè alcuni prestiti, uno dopo l'altro: «Se credi, se proprio vuoi, se puoi ...» aveva detto ogni volta, guardando a terra, con quel suo fare che pareva incerto, e forse non era, con quel suo stile tentennante, tergiversante: pure, il circolare assegno della «banca d'interesse nazionale»[19] (una delle cinque) gli era sparito tra i diti in men che non si dice, ogni volta in un soffio: come il re di picche tra le digitanti dita di un mago.

Eucarpio, nel suo buon cuore, meditò il fattibile: se-

Among his ex-school-fellows, among those most dear to his heart, was Prosdocimo: to whom Eucarpio felt himself bound by a brotherly friendship. But Prosdocimo's life, with the Second World War, or perhaps even before, had taken a wrong turning. In the first place ... he had gone to live in another town, much less industrious than that referred to above, in which they had both declined Latin nouns at school. He had left a remunerative and very worth-while job in order to spend his time on trifles. He had been ill with stomach trouble: had given up the idea of marrying: and lived alone; as, people say, the owl likes living: (which is not true, for even the owl takes a wife). He lived in what he said was a miserable attic: a fine pent-house, in reality, constructed by the landlord himself, who was an engineer of great merit, having been, it is true, a General in the Corps of Engineers. The rain came through the ceiling, but that is beside the point. Prosdocimo enjoyed a poor reputation with the neighbours: if a servant-girl sang, of a morning, or a dog howled at the moon from some deserted back garden, he would indulge in shocking displays of bad temper. And then he had not a penny left. And then he was mad. On this point Eucarpio, who was a man of great perspicacity, as has been explained, by now had no doubt. However, in his equally great goodness of heart, he had not hesitated to offer his friend some help in confronting the privations and hardship of life after the rain of bombs, while waiting for the 'promised reconstruction' of the city.

Prosdocimo had, unexpectedly, accepted the subsidies, or rather, a few loans, one after the other: 'If you think so, if you really insist, if you can afford it ...' he had said each time, his eyes downcast, with that way of his that seemed uncertain, and perhaps was not; his manner diffident, evasive: anyhow, the order from the Bank of National Interest (one of the five important ones) disappeared through his fingers in no time, like a whiff of air, on each occasion: as the King of Spades disappears between the dexterous fingers of a conjurer.

Eucarpio, in his warm-hearted way, considered what was

guitò intanto a esercitare l'acume che l'aveva provveduto fin là: trovò che il rimedio di tutti i mali, per Prosdocimo, sarebbe stato ... il gran toccasana del matrimonio. Ma, dato che era pazzo, chi proporgli? Quale vittima offrire ... a un così biscornuto[20] Minotauro?

A ventidue anni (l'età in cui Renzo, come a Dio piacque, impalmò la Lucia)[21] nessuno aveva proposto una moglie a Prosdocimo. C'era l'Adamello, allora, che lo aspettava: l'Altipiano dei Sette Comuni, il Carso, il Sabotino e l'Isonzo.[22] Là, forse, avrebbe trovato la sposa: quella che non fa le corna a nessuno, e a tutti di giorno in giorno le fa. Ma non la trovò neppur là. Anzi, tra quei sassi, e un rovinio di folgori, cominciò a capire che nessuna lo voleva. Neppur la sposa del Carso lo volle: preferì mille altri.

Avvenne che nella città meno industre in cui era, per dir così, andato a sbattere, – bombardato, mitragliato, spezzonato e preso a cannonate un po' da tutti, tra gli anni vecchi di Cecco Beppe[23] e i nuovi ed insigni dell'Adolfa,[24] tra la tana di neve dell'Adamello e il sopralzo acquatico del generale del genio – avvenne che in quella villa ci si radicasse pure una signora, della quale tanto lui quanto Eucarpio erano stati, illis temporibus, cioè sui banchi del ginnasio, ammiratori giovinetti. Dice infatti l'Ariosto «ch'a trovar si vanno gli uomini spesso e i monti fermi stanno».[25] Gli uomini, e le donne. I casi della vita portarono la signora Eulalia, vedova fulgente, nella città meno industre: dove, spesso, le occorreva di prendere il treno, in direzione della più industre.

Quando Eucarpio, per una felicissima combinazione, la incontrò sul rapido, mutò il posto con lo sbigottito colonnello che le sedeva dirimpetto. E seppe ... tutto! Che Prosdocimo era stato da lei sorpreso alla Ù.P.I.M.[26] nell'attò di perpetrare il verecondo acquisto ... di un

feasible: continuing meanwhile to exert the acumen that so far had served him well: and came to the conclusion that the remedy for all the ills of Prosdocimo would be ... the great panacea of matrimony. But, given that he was mad, who could be proposed for him? What victim should be offered up ... to so oddly-horned a Minotaur?

When twenty-two years old (the age at which, by God's will, Renzo had won Lucia's hand) no one had suggested a wife for Prosdocimo. It was the Monte Adamello, then, that awaited him: the uplands of the Seven Communes, the Carso, the Sabotino, and the Isonzo. There, perhaps, he might have found his bride: the bride who cuckolds no one, and by whom, day by day, all men are cuckolded. But he did not find her even there. Indeed, amongst those rocks, and the crash of thunder, he came to understand that he was wanted by nobody. Not even the bride of the Carso would have him: she preferred a thousand others.

It happened that in that less industrious city in which he had, so to speak, landed himself – bombed, machine-gunned, blown up, bombarded more or less by everyone, between the last years of Franz Joseph and those, new and notable, of the Hitlerian wild beast; between the snow-bound dug-outs of the Adamello and the dripping pent-house of the General of Engineers – it happened that in that same house a lady, too, had taken root, of whom both he and Eucarpio had been, *illis temporibus,* in other words, when at school, youthful admirers. Ariosto, in fact, says, that 'men often go to meet one another and the mountains stay where they are'. Men, and women, too. The ups and downs of life brought the Signora Eulalia, a widow of effulgent charms, to the less industrious city: from which she often had occasion to take the train, in the direction of the more industrious one.

When Eucarpio, by a most happy coincidence, met her in the express, he made the astonished colonel who was sitting opposite her change places with him. And learned ... all! That she had taken Prosdocimo by surprise in the U.P.I.M. in the act of making the embarrassing acquisition

paio di bretelle. (Risero: la signora con una risata ampia, gioconda, piena di bellissimi denti.) Agli inviti reiterati della gentile ex-condiscepola, l'acquirente di elastici aveva, more solito, nicchiato, tergiversato, tentennato, traccheggiato, indugiato e risposto ni: cioè sì: cioè no: e poi non c'era andato del tutto. Tanto che lei, sdegnata, s'era poi stufata d'invitarlo. S'era sprangato in casa atterrito, come Don Abbondio dopo il fatale incontro coi due.[27]

Eucarpio . . . Voi che cos'avreste fatto? Be', lui prese il treno a sua volta e andò a stanare[28] quel pazzo: e gne ne[29] disse. Gli disse: «Vergognati. Quello che stai combinando non lo so, non mi risulta: e non m'interessa di saperlo. So, comunque, che non è degno di un uomo,» così disse: «che non è degno del mio amico, del mio vecchio compagno. Consumi gli ultimi risparmi, e gli ultimi anni, senza concluder nulla. Morirai nella neve.[30] I miei aiuti non possono continuare all'infinito. Il tuo contegno è quello di un demente. La tua anomalia psichica, che è indiscutibile . . .»

«Perché indiscutibile? . . .» chiese tristemente Prosdocimo.

«Perché sì. Lasciami dire. La tua anomalia psichica, dicevo, non interrompermi!, ti serve magnificamente a pretesto per gabbare il prossimo . . .»

«Una causa vera non può essere un pretesto . . .»

«È vera, ma è anche un pretesto. Tu sfrutti il tuo male per gabbare il mondo: per farti beffe di tutti . . .»

«Gabbare il mo . . .? E come, e chi ho mai gabbato? . . .» cercò invano, per entro lo strazio della sua memoria, un qualche cosa che si potesse chiamare aver gabbato qualcheduno.

«Hai gabbato un po' tutti: hai deluso[31] tutti. Tutte le persone serie. Tutti quelli che t'hanno conceduto la loro stima: che avevano ragione di aspettarsi, in cambio, qualche cosa da te . . . e oggi se ne pentono! . . .»

«Male, se aspettavano,» ebbe la faccia di rispondere. «Io non aspetto niente da loro. Ho le ossa rotte[32] . . . non

of . . . a pair of braces. (They laughed: the signora had a full, joyous laugh, showing fine teeth.) At the reiterated invitations of his kindly ex-school-fellow the buyer of elastic had, in his usual way, hesitated, hummed and ha'd, wavered, vacillated and temporized, replying n'yes: that is, yes: that is, no: and then he had not gone at all. So that she, offended, had got tired of asking him. He had locked himself up at home, terrified, like Don Abbondio after his fatal meeting with the two bravoes.

Eucarpio . . . And what would you have done? Well, he took the train in his turn and went to dig out that madman from his den: and gave him a piece of his mind. He said: 'You ought to be ashamed of yourself. I don't know what you're up to, it's not clear to me: and I don't want to know. But anyhow,' he said, 'I know that it's not worthy of a man, of my friend, of my old school-fellow. You are using up your last savings, your last years, without achieving anything. You'll die in the gutter. My help can't go on for ever. Your behaviour is that of a lunatic. Your psychological oddness, which is unquestionable . . .'

'Why unquestionable?' asked Prosdocimo, sadly.

'Because it is. Let me speak. Your psychological oddness, as I said – don't interrupt! – serves you splendidly as a pretext for deluding your neighbours . . .'

'A true cause can't be a pretext . . .'

'It is a true one, but it is also a pretext. You exploit your malady to trick people: to take everyone in . . .'

'To trick pe . . .? And how, whom have I ever tricked? . . .' He sought in vain, amid the torment of his memories, for something that could be described as tricking anybody.

'You've deceived everyone, more or less: you've disappointed everyone. All serious-minded people. All those who had a good opinion of you: who had reason to expect something from you, in return . . . and regret it now! . . .'

'It's unfortunate, if they were expecting anything,' he had the face to reply. 'I expect nothing from them. I'm done

sono responsabile della loro ... serietà ...» E guardò fuori. Scheletri di generalizie case apparivano, folgorate, sul sempiterno sfondo del colle: una torricella stupenda, in stile floreale, era il cacatoio[33] dei colombi.

Eucarpio guardò lui: s'infuriò. Tanta insolenza, davvero, passava il segno del credibile.

«Ora basta! Eccoti le ultime quattromila lire che ti devo: a regolazione delle nostre pendenze. Ma non sperar più un soldo da me. E permettimi di dirti ... che ... se continui così ...», Prosdocimo lo guardò atterrito (d'un terrore simulato), palpò, con simulata noncuranza, il peperonetto bistorto, polipuntuto, di corallo scarlatto,[34] che arditamente gli fuoruscíva dal gilè: «... finirai male. È inutile che ti palpi il tuo corno. Non è un augurio, il mio. È una constatazione matematica ...» Prosdocimo, a ogni buon conto, palpò e ripalpò, giocherellò e rigiocherellò con le dita quel fregnetto.[35] «Piantala, scemo!... Se vai avanti così finirai male ...»

«E può darsi. Tutti, quando s'ha da finire, si finisce poco bene ..»

Eucarpio, distratto, vinto da quella caparbietà così ottusa, parve raccattare un pensiero.

«... La nostra compagna di scuola! Una donna come lei! Così bella, così generosa! Una donna della sua intelligenza! Di cui tu stesso eri innamorato, si può dire, quando eri un altro, quando eri te stesso ...»

«Un altro, o me stesso? ...»

«Quando non eri ancora uno scemo ... Quel Prosdocimo a cui ho dato la mia stima, l'amicizia di tant'anni ... A cui ho voluto bene: negli anni ... in cui non si poteva evitare di volerti bene ... in cui lei stessa te ne ha voluto, forse ...»

«Sì, forse. Trentotto anni fa ...»

for ... I'm not responsible for their ... serious-mindedness ...'

He looked out of the window. The skeletons of houses belonging to the General appeared, stricken, against the eternal background of the hills: a fine little bell-tower, decorated in *art-nouveau* style, was foul with the excrement of pigeons.

Eucarpio looked at him: and became enraged. Such insolence really passed the bounds of credibility.

'That's enough! Here are the last four thousand *lire* that I owe you: in settlement of our account. But don't expect another penny from me. And allow me to tell you ... that ... if you go on like this ...', Prosdocimo looked at him, terrorstruck (with simulated terror), and fingered, with simulated carelessness, the small, many-pointed amulet of scarlet coral, shaped like a red pepper, that protruded, daringly, from his waistcoat: '... you will come to a bad end. It's no use your fiddling with that thing. I'm not *wishing* you a bad end. It's a mathematical certainty ...' Prosdocimo's fingers, just to make sure, were repeatedly patting and playing with his little charm against the Evil Eye. 'Stop it, you fool! ... If you go on like this, you *will* come to a bad end ...'

'Very likely. We all, when it comes to the end, finish up none too well ...'

Eucarpio, unheeding, and defeated by a stubbornness so obtuse, seemed to catch at a sudden thought.

'... Our school-friend! A woman like her! So handsome, so generous! A woman of her intelligence! With whom you yourself were in love, one might say, when you were another, when you were yourself ...'

'Another, or myself?'

'When you weren't yet an idiot.... That Prosdocimo to whom I gave my esteem, my friendship, for so many years. ... Whom I loved ... in those years ... when one couldn't help loving you ... when she herself loved you, maybe ...'

'Yes, maybe. Thirty-eight years ago ...'

«Vergognati!» s'infuriò Eucarpio a quel trentotto.
«Vergognati. Dovresti sposarla. Ecco quel che farei,
io, se fossi al tuo posto . . . La sposerei. Ma capisco bene
ch'è fatica sprecata, la mia: vox clamantis . . .[36]»

«Ante porcos . . .»

«Non imbrogliar le carte anche a Cristo. Non degra-
darti fino a questo punto. Contentati di essere quell'anomalo psichico che sei . . . È già molto . . .»

Prosdocimo, quella sera, contro ogni abitudine, com-
però dugentocinquantasei[37] lire di cognac. Poi si sprangò
in casa: (un tremendo colpo di catenaccio, i casigliani
sussultarono). Poi palpò il corno: trentadue volte. Trentadue è la quinta potenza di due, dugentocinquantasei
l'ottava. Due è il numero genetico: dalle amebe ai mam-
miferi, all'homo sapiens. Cinque è numero perfetto, e
dodici altrettanto, secondo la gnosi dei pitagorici. Poi
contò e ricontò quattro biglietti da mille: come fossero
stati quattrocento. Poi li baciò. Vi aggiunse novantasei
lire da far quattromila e novantasei, che è la dodicesima
potenza di due, numero generativo (dei biglietti da mille).
Poi ribaciò il tutto: e nascose quel valsente nel «Tractatus
de lapide philosophico» di San Tommaso d'Aquino: poi
mutò idea e lo mise invece nelle «Confessioni» di Gian
Giacomo.[38] Poi, siccome la serva di due piani sotto la
sfringuellava al telefono coll'innamorato, assenti i padroni, si imbizzì: prese a pestare i piedi sacripantando «porca, porca, porca, porca[39] . . .»: finché la non ismise, che
non fu molto presto. Allora si risovvenne del cognac: lo
tracannò d'un fiato, a garganella, come dal poppatoio
un bambinaccio. Sedé al tavolo, accese la lampada: si
diede una fregatina di mani: principiò a canterellare,
tonitruando, mentre abbadava a riempir la penna
malvagia: «Anomalo psichico, anomalo psichico . . .»

Tra le ceneri delle battaglie lontane . . .

'You ought to be ashamed!' Eucarpio fumed at that thirty-eight. 'Ashamed. You ought to marry her. That's what I would do in your place. I'd marry her. But I know it's a waste of time, talking to you: *vox clamantis* ...'

'*Ante porcos* ...'

'Don't try your trickery on Christ, too. Don't degrade yourself that far. Be content with remaining the psychological oddity you are. It's quite enough ...'

That evening Prosdocimo, against all his usual habits, spent two hundred and fifty-six *lire* on brandy. Then he locked himself into his pent-house: (a terrific clanging of bolts startled the other tenants). Then he patted his coral charm thirty-two times. Thirty-two is the fifth power of two, and two hundred and fifty-six is the eighth. Two is the genetic number: from the amoebae to the mammals and to *homo sapiens*. Five is a perfect number, and so is twelve, according to the gnosis of the Pythagoreans. Then he counted and re-counted the four one-thousand-*lire* notes: as if they had been four hundred. Then he kissed them. He added ninety-six *lire* to make four thousand and ninety-six, which is the twelfth power of two, the generative number (of thousand-*lire* notes). Then he kissed the whole lot once more: and hid this capital-sum in the *Tractatus de lapide philosophico* of Saint Thomas Aquinas: but changed his mind and put it instead in the *Confessions* of Jean-Jacques. Then, because the servant-girl two floors down was chattering at the telephone with her young man, her employers being away, he lost his temper: and began to stamp his feet, bellowing 'Bitch, bitch, bitch, bitch ...' until she gave up, which was not very soon. Then he remembered the brandy: and gulped it down in one draught, from the flask, like a greedy child at the feeding-bottle. Sitting down at the table, he lit the lamp: rubbed his hands: and began to chant to himself, in a toneless voice, while trying to fill his refractory pen: 'Psychological oddity, psychological oddity ...'

Amid the ashes of battles long ago ...

THE MOTHER
NATALIA GINZBURG

Translated by Isabel Quigly

LA MADRE

La madre era piccola e magra, con le spalle un po' curve;
portava sempre una sottana blu e una blusa di lana rossa.
Aveva i capelli neri crespi e corti, li ungeva sempre con
dell'olio perché non stessero tanto gonfi; ogni giorno si
strappava le sopracciglia, ne faceva due pesciolini neri
che guizzavano verso le tempie; s'incipriava il viso di
una cipria gialla. Era molto giovane; quanti anni avesse
loro non sapevano ma pareva tanto piú giovane delle
madri dei loro compagni di scuola; i ragazzi si stupivano
sempre a vedere le madri dei loro compagni, com'erano
grasse e vecchie. Fumava molto e aveva le dita macchiate
dal fumo; fumava anche la sera a letto, prima d'addormentarsi. Dormivano tutti e tre insieme, nel grande letto
matrimoniale con la trapunta gialla; la madre stava dal
lato della porta, sul comodino aveva una lampada col
paralume fasciato d'un cencio rosso, perché la notte
leggeva e fumava; certe volte rientrava molto tardi, i
ragazzi si svegliavano allora e le chiedevano dove era
stata: lei quasi sempre rispondeva: – Al cinema –,
oppure: – Da una mia amica –; chi fosse quest'amica non
sapevano perché nessuna amica era mai venuta a casa a
trovare la madre. Lei diceva loro che dovevano voltarsi
dall'altra mentre si spogliava, sentivano il fruscio veloce
degli abiti, sui muri ballavano ombre; s'infilava nel letto
accanto a loro, magro corpo nella fredda camicia di seta,
si mettevano discosti da lei perché sempre si lamentava
che le stavano addosso e le davano calci nel sonno; qualche volta spegneva la luce perché loro s'addormentassero
e fumava zitta nell'ombra.
   La madre non era importante. Era importante la nonna, il nonno, la zia Clementina che abitava in campagna
e arrivava ogni tanto con castagne e farina gialla; era im-

THE MOTHER

Their mother was small and thin, and slightly round-shouldered; she always wore a blue skirt and a red woollen blouse. She had short, curly black hair which she kept oiled to control its bushiness; every day she plucked her eyebrows, making two black fish of them that swam towards her temples; and she used yellow powder on her face. She was very young; how old, they didn't know, but she seemed much younger than the mothers of the boys at school; they were always surprised to see their friends' mothers, how old and fat they were. She smoked a great deal and her fingers were stained with smoke; she even smoked in bed in the evening, before going to sleep. All three of them slept together, in the big double bed with the yellow quilt; their mother was on the side nearest the door, and on the bedside table she had a lamp with its shade wrapped in a red cloth, because at night she read and smoked; sometimes she came in very late, and the boys would wake up and ask her where she had been: she nearly always answered: 'At the cinema', or else 'With a girl friend of mine'; who this friend was they didn't know, because no woman friend had ever been to the house to see their mother. She told them they must turn the other way while she undressed, they heard the quick rustle of her clothes, and shadows danced on the walls; she slipped into bed beside them, her thin body in its cold silk nightdress, and they moved away from her because she always complained that they came too close and kicked while they slept; sometimes she put out the light so that they should go to sleep and smoked in silence in the darkness.

Their mother was not important. Granny, Grandpa, Aunt Clementina who lived in the country and turned up now and then with chestnuts and maize-flour were impor-

portante Diomira, la serva, era importante Giovanni, il
portinaio tisico che faceva delle sedie di paglia; tutte queste persone erano molto importanti per i due ragazzi perché erano gente forte di cui ci si poteva fidare, gente forte
nel permettere e nel proibire, molto bravi in tutte le cose
che facevano e pieni sempre di saggezza e di forza; gente
che poteva difendere dai temporali e dai ladri. Ma se
erano in casa con la madre i ragazzi avevano paura proprio come se fossero stati soli; quanto al permettere e al
proibire lei non permetteva né proibiva mai nulla, al
massimo si lamentava con una voce stanca: – Non fate
tanto chiasso perché io ho mal di testa –, e se le doman-
davano il permesso di fare una cosa o l'altra lei subito
rispondeva: – Chiedete alla nonna –, oppure diceva
prima no e poi sí e poi no ed era tutta una confusione.
Quando uscivano soli con la madre si sentivano incerti e
malsicuri perché lei sempre sbagliava le strade e bisognava
domandare al vigile e aveva poi un modo cosí buffo e
timido di entrare nei negozi a chiedere le cose da comprare, e nei negozi dimenticava sempre qualcosa, i guanti
o la borsetta o la sciarpa, e bisognava tornare indietro a
cercare e i ragazzi avevano vergogna.

La madre teneva i cassetti in disordine e lasciava tutte
le cose in giro e Diomira al mattino quando rifaceva la
stanza brontolava contro di lei. Chiamava anche la nonna
a vedere e insieme raccoglievano calze e abiti e scopavano
via la cenere che era sparsa un po' dappertutto. La madre
al mattino andava a fare la spesa: tornava e sbatteva la
rete sul tavolo di marmo in cucina e pigliava la sua bicicletta e correva all'ufficio dov'era impiegata. Diomira
guardava tutto quello che c'era nella rete, toccava gli
aranci a uno a uno e la carne, e brontolava e chiamava la
nonna a vedere com'era brutta la carne. La madre ritor-
nava a casa alle due quando loro tutti avevano già mangiato e mangiava in fretta col giornale appoggiato al bicchiere e poi filava via in bicicletta di nuovo all'ufficio e
la rivedevano un momento a cena, ma dopo cena quasi
sempre filava via.

tant; Diomira the maid was important, Giovanni the tuber-
cular porter who made cane chairs was important; all these
were very important to the two boys because they were strong
people you could trust, strong people in allowing and for-
bidding, very good at everything they did and always full of
wisdom and strength; people who could defend you from
storms and robbers. But if they were at home with their
mother the boys were frightened, just as if they had been
alone; as for allowing or forbidding, she never allowed or
forbade anything, at the most she complained in a weary
voice: 'Don't make such a row because I've got a headache,'
and if they asked permission to do something or other she
answered at once: 'Ask Granny', or she said no first and
then yes and then no and it was all a muddle. When they
went out alone with their mother they felt uncertain and
insecure because she always took wrong turnings and had
to ask a policeman the way, and then she had such a funny,
timid way of going into shops to ask for things to buy, and
in the shops she always forgot something, gloves or handbag
or scarf, and had to go back to look and the boys were
ashamed.

Their mother's drawers were untidy and she left all her
things scattered about and Diomira grumbled about her
when she did out the room in the morning. She even called
Granny in to see and together they picked up stockings and
clothes and swept up the ash that was scattered all over the
place. In the morning their mother went to do the shopping: she came back and flung the string bag on the marble
table in the kitchen and took her bicycle and dashed off to
the office where she worked. Diomira looked at all the
things in the string bag, touched the oranges one by one and
the meat, and grumbled and called Granny to see what poor
meat it was. Their mother came home at two o'clock when
they had all eaten and ate quickly with the newspaper
propped up against her glass and then rushed off again to
the office on her bicycle and they saw her for a minute at
supper again, but after supper she nearly always dashed off.

LA MADRE

I ragazzi facevano i compiti nella stanza da letto. C'era il ritratto del padre, grande, a capo del letto, con la quadrata barba nera e la testa calva e gli occhiali cerchiati di tartaruga, e poi un altro suo ritrattino sul tavolo, con in collo il minore dei ragazzi. Il padre era morto quando loro erano molto piccoli, non ricordavano nulla di lui: o meglio c'era nella memoria del ragazzo piú grande l'ombra d'un pomeriggio lontanissimo, in campagna dalla zia Clementina: il padre lo spingeva sul prato in una carriola verde; aveva trovato poi qualche pezzo di quella carriola, un manico e una ruota, in soffitta dalla zia Clementina; nuova era una bellissima carriola e lui era felice di averla; il padre lo spingeva correndo e la sua lunga barba svolazzava. Non sapevano niente del padre ma pensavano che doveva essere del tipo di quelli che son forti e saggi nel permettere e nel proibire: la nonna quando il nonno o Diomira si arrabbiavano contro la madre diceva che bisognava aver pietà di lei perché era stata molto disgraziata e diceva che se ci fosse stato Eugenio, il padre dei ragazzi, sarebbe stata tutt'un'altra donna, ma invece aveva avuto quella disgrazia di perdere il marito quando era ancora giovane. C'era stata per un certo tempo anche la nonna paterna, non l'avevano mai veduta perché abitava in Francia ma scriveva e mandava dei regalini a Natale: poi aveva finito col morire perché era molto vecchia.

A merenda mangiavano castagne, o pane con l'olio e l'aceto, e poi se avevano finito il compito potevano scendere a giocare in piazzetta o fra le rovine dei bagni pubblici, saltati in aria in un bombardamento. In piazzetta c'erano molti piccioni e loro gli portavano del pane o si facevano dare da Diomira un cartoccio di riso avanzato. Là s'incontravano con tutti i ragazzi del quartiere, compagni di scuola e altri che ritrovavano poi al ricreatorio la domenica, quando facevano le partite al pallone con don Vigliani che si tirava su la sottana nera e tirava calci. Anche in piazzetta a volte giocavano al pallone o giocavano a ladri e carabinieri. La nonna di tanto in tanto si

The boys did their homework in the bedroom. There was their father's picture, large at the head of the bed, with his square black beard and bald head and tortoiseshell-rimmed spectacles, and then another small portrait on the table, with the younger of the boys in his arms. Their father had died when they were very small, they remembered nothing about him: or rather in the older boy's memory there was the shadow of a very distant afternoon, in the country at Aunt Clementina's: his father was pushing him across the meadow in a green wheelbarrow; afterwards he had found some pieces of this wheelbarrow, a handle and a wheel, in Aunt Clementina's attic; when it was new it was a splendid wheelbarrow and he was glad to have it; his father ran along pushing him and his long beard flapped. They knew nothing about their father but they thought he must be the sort of person who is strong and wise in allowing and for-bidding; when Grandpa or Diomira got angry with their mother Granny said that they should be sorry for her be-cause she had been very unfortunate, and she said that if Eugenio, the boys' father, had been there she would have been an entirely different woman, whereas she had had the misfortune to lose her husband when she was still young. For a time there had been their father's mother as well, they never saw her because she lived in France but she used to write and send Christmas presents: then in the end she died because she was very old.

At tea-time they ate chestnuts, or bread with oil and vinegar, and then if they had finished their homework they could go and play in the small piazza or among the ruins of the public baths, which had been blown up in an air raid. In the small piazza there were a great many pigeons and they took them bread or got Diomira to give them a paper bag of left-over rice. There they met all the local boys, boys from school and others they met in the youth clubs on Sundays when they had football matches with Don Vigliani, who hitched up his black cassock and kicked. Sometimes they played football in the small piazza too or else cops and robbers. Their grandmother appeared on the balcony

affacciava al balcone e gridava di non farsi male: era bello vedere dalla piazza buia le finestre illuminate della casa, là al terzo piano, e sapere che si poteva ritornare là, scaldarsi alla stufa e difendersi dalla notte. La nonna sedeva in cucina con Diomira e rammendavano le lenzuola; il nonno stava nella stanza da pranzo e fumava la pipa col berretto in testa. La nonna era molto grassa, vestita di nero, e portava al petto un medaglione col ritratto dello zio Oreste che era morto in guerra: era molto brava a cucinare le pizze e altre cose. La nonna li prendeva qualche volta sulle ginocchia, anche adesso che erano abbastanza grandi; era grassa, aveva un grande petto tutto molle: si vedeva da sotto lo scollo dell'abito nero la grossa maglia di lana bianca col bordo a festoni che si era fata da sè. Li prendeva sulle ginocchia e diceva nel suo dialetto delle parole tenere e come un poco pietose; e poi si tirava fuori dalla crocchia una lunga forcina di ferro e gli puliva le orecchie, e loro strillavano e volevano scappare e veniva sulla porta il nonno con la sua pipa.

Il nonno era prima professore di greco e di latino al liceo.[1] Adesso era in pensione e scriveva una grammatica greca: molti dei suoi antichi studenti venivano ogni tanto a trovarlo. Diomira allora doveva fare il caffè; c'erano al cesso fogli di quaderno con versioni dal latino e dal greco, con le sue correzioni in rosso e blu. Il nonno aveva una barbetta bianca, un po' come quella d'una capra, e non bisognava for chiasso perché lui aveva i nervi stanchi da tanti anni che aveva fatto la scuola; era sempre un po' spaventato perché i prezzi crescevano e la nonna doveva sempre un po' litigare con lui al mattino, perché si stupiva sempre del denaro che ci voleva; diceva che forse Diomira rubava lo zucchero e si faceva il caffè di nascosto e Diomira allora sentiva e correva da lui a gridare, il caffè era per gli studenti che venivano sempre; ma questi erano piccoli incidenti che si quietavano subito e i ragazzi non si spaventavano, invece si spaventavano quando c'era una lite fra il nonno e la madre; succedeva certe volte se

occasionally and called to them not to get hurt: it was nice
seeing the lighted windows of their home, up there on the
third floor, from the dark piazza, and knowing that they
could go back there, warm up at the stove and guard themselves from the night. Granny sat in the kitchen with
Diomira and mended the linen; Grandpa was in the dining-
room with his cap on, smoking his pipe. Granny was very
fat, and wore black, and on her breast a medal with a picture of Uncle Oreste who had died in the war: she was very
good at cooking pizzas and things. Sometimes she took them
on her knee, even now when they were quite big boys; she
was fat, she had a large soft bosom; from under the neck
of her black dress you could see the thick white woollen vest
with a scolloped edge which she had made herself. She
would take them on her knee and say tender and slightly
pitiful-sounding words in dialect; then she would take a
long iron hair-pin out of her bun and clean their ears, and
they would shriek and try to get away and Grandpa would
come to the door with his pipe.

Grandpa had taught Greek and Latin at the high school.
Now he was pensioned off and was writing a Greek grammar: many of his old pupils used to come and see him now
and then. Then Diomira would make coffee; in the lava-
tory there were exercise book pages with Latin and Greek
unseens on them, and his corrections in red and blue.
Grandpa had a small white beard, a sort of goatee, and they
were not to make a racket because his nerves were tired
after all those years at school; he was always rather alarmed
because prices kept going up and Granny always had a bit
of a row with him in the morning because he was always
surprised at the money they needed; he would say that perhaps Diomira pinched the sugar and made coffee in secret
and Diomira would hear and rush at him and yell that the
coffee was for the students who kept coming; but these were
small incidents that quietened down at once and the boys
were not alarmed, whereas they were alarmed when there
was a quarrel between Grandpa and their mother; this

la madre rientrava molto tardi la notte, lui allora veniva
fuori dalla sua stanza col cappotto sopra il pigiama e a
piedi scalzi, e gridavano lui e la madre: lui diceva: – Lo
so dove sei stata, lo so dove sei stata, lo so chi sei – e
la madre diceva: – Cosa me ne importa –, e diceva: –
Ecco, guarda che m'hai svegliato i bambini –, e lui diceva: – Per quello che te ne importa dei tuoi bambini.
Non parlare perché lo so chi sei. Una cagna sei. Te ne
corri in giro la notte da quella cagna pazza che sei –. E
allora venivano fuori la nonna e Diomira in camicia e lo
spingevano nella sua stanza e facevano: «Sss, sss» e la
madre s'infilava nel letto e singhiozzava sotto le lenzuola,
i suoi alti singhiozzi risuonavano nella stanza buia: i ragazzi pensavano che il nonno certo aveva ragione, pensavano che la madre faceva male a andare al cinema e dalle
amiche la notte. Si sentivano molto infelici, spaventati e
infelici, se ne stavano rannicchiati vicini nel caldo letto
morbido e profondo, e il ragazzo piú grande che era al
centro si stringeva da parte per non toccare il corpo della
madre: gli pareva che ci fosse qualcosa di schifoso nel
pianto della madre, nel guanciale bagnato: pensava: «Un
ragazzo ha schifo di sua madre quando lei piange». Di
queste liti della madre col nonno non parlavano mai fra
loro, evitavano accuratamente di parlarne: ma si volevano molto bene[2] tra loro e stavano abbracciati stretti la
notte quando la madre piangeva: al mattino si vergognavano un po' uno dell'altro, perché si erano abbracciati
cosí stretti come per difendersi e perché c'era quella cosa
di cui non volevano parlare; d'altronde si dimenticavano
presto d'essere stati infelici, il giorno cominciava e sarebbero andati a scuola, e per la strada avrebbero trovato i
compagni e giocato un momento sulla porta della scuola.
　Nella luce grigia del mattino, la madre si alzava: col
sottabito arrotolato alla vita, s'insaponava il collo e le
braccia stando curva sulla catinella: cercava sempre di
non farsi vedere da loro ma scorgevano nello specchio le
sue spalle brune e scarne e le piccole mammelle nude:
nel freddo i capezzoli si facevano scuri e sporgenti, solle-

happened sometimes if their mother came home very late at night, he would come out of his room with his overcoat over his pyjamas and bare feet, and he and their mother would shout: he said: 'I know where you've been, I know where you've been, I know what you are,' and their mother said: 'What do I care?' and then: 'Look, now you've woken the children,' and he said: 'A fat lot you care what happens to your children. Don't say anything because I know what you are. You're a bitch. You run around at night like the mad bitch you are.' And then Granny and Diomira would come out in their nightdresses and push him into his room and say: 'Shush, shush,' and their mother would get into bed and sob under the bedclothes, her deep sobs echoing in the dark room: the boys thought that Grandpa must be right, they thought their mother was wrong to go to the cinema and to her girl friends at night. They felt very unhappy, frightened and unhappy, and lay huddled close together in the deep, warm, soft bed, and the older boy who was in the middle pushed away so as not to touch his mother's body: there seemed to him something disgusting in his mother's tears, in the wet pillow: he thought: 'It gives a chap the creeps when his mother cries.' They never spoke between themselves of these rows their mother and Grandpa had, they carefully avoided mentioning them: but they loved each other very much and clung close together at night when their mother cried: in the morning they were faintly embarrassed, because they had hugged so tightly as if to protect themselves, and because there was that thing they didn't want to talk about; besides, they soon forgot that they had been unhappy, the day began and they went to school, and met their friends in the street, and played for a moment at the school door.

In the grey light of morning, their mother got up: with her petticoat wound round her waist she soaped her neck and arms standing bent over the basin: she always tried not to let them see her but in the looking glass they could make out her thin brown shoulders and small naked breasts: in the cold the nipples became dark and protruding, she raised

vava le braccia e s'incipriava le ascelle: alle ascelle aveva
dei peli ricciuti e folti. Quando era tutta vestita cominciava a strapparsi le sopracciglia, fissandosi nello specchio da vicino e stringendo forte le labbra: poi si spal-
mava il viso d'una crema e scuoteva forte il piumino di
cigno color rosa acceso e s'incipriava: il suo viso diventava allora tutto giallo. Certe volte era abbastanza allegra
al mattino e voleva parlare coi ragazzi, chiedeva della
scuola e dei compagni e raccontava qualcosa del tempo
che lei era a scuola: aveva una maestra che si chiamava
«signorina Dirce» ed era una vecchia zitella che voleva
fare la giovane. Poi s'infilava il cappotto e pigliava la rete
della spesa, si chinava a baciare i ragazzi e correva via
con la sciarpa avvolta intorno al capo e col suo viso tutto
profumato e incipriato di cipria gialla.

I ragazzi trovavano strano d'esser nati da lei. Sarebbe
stato molto meno strano nascere dalla nonna o da Diomira, con quel loro grandi corpi caldi che proteggevano
dalla paura, che difendevano dai temporali e dai ladri.
Era molto strano pensare che la loro madre era quella,
che lei li aveva contenuti un tempo nel suo piccolo ventre.
Da quando avevano saputo che i bambini stanno nella
pancia della madre prima di nascere, si erano sentiti molto stupiti e anche un po' vergognosi che quel ventre li
avesse contenuti un tempo. E anche gli aveva dato il latte
con le sue mammelle: e questo era ancora piú inverosi-
mile. Ma adesso non aveva piú figli piccoli da allattare e
cullare, e ogni giorno la vedevano filare via in bicicletta
dopo la spesa con uno scatto libero e felice del corpo.
Lei non apparteneva certo a loro: non potevano contare
su di lei. Non potevano chiederle nulla: c'erano altre madri, le madri dei loro compagni, a cui era chiaro che si
poteva chiedere un mondo di cose; i compagni correvano
dalle madri dopo ch'era finita la scuola e chiedevano un
mondo di cose, si facevano soffiare il naso e abbottonare il
cappotto, mostravano i compiti e i giornaletti: queste madri erano abbastanza vecchie, con dei cappelli o con delle
velette o con baveri di pelliccia e venivano quasi ogni

her arms and powdered her armpits: in her armpits she had thick curly hair. When she was completely dressed she started plucking her eyebrows, staring at herself in the mirror from close to and biting her lips hard: then she smothered her face with cream and shook the pink swansdown puff hard and powdered herself: then her face became all yellow. Sometimes she was quite gay in the mornings and wanted to talk to the boys, she asked them about school and their friends and told them things about her time at school: she had a teacher called 'Signorina Dirce' and she was an old maid who tried to seem young. Then she put on her coat and picked up her string shopping bag, leant down to kiss the boys and ran out with her scarf wound round her head and her face all perfumed and powdered with yellow powder.

The boys thought it strange to have been born of her. It would have been much less strange to have been born of Granny or Diomira, with their large warm bodies that protected you from fear, that defended you from storms and robbers. It was very strange to think she was their mother, that she had held them for a while in her small womb. Since they learnt that children are in their mother's tummy before being born, they had felt very surprised and also a little ashamed that that womb had once held them. And that she had given them milk from her breasts as well: this was even more unlikely. But now she no longer had small children to feed and cradle, and every day they saw her dash off on her bicycle when the shopping was done, her body jerking away, free and happy. She certainly didn't belong to them: they couldn't count on her. You couldn't ask her anything: there were other mothers, the mothers of their school friends, whom clearly you could ask about all sorts of things; their friends ran to their mothers when school was over and asked them heaps of things, got their noses blown and their overcoats buttoned, showed their homework and their comics: these mothers were pretty old, with hats or veils or fur collars and they came to talk to the master practically every

giorno a parlare con il maestro: erano gente come la nonna o come Diomira, grandi corpi mansueti e imperiosi di
gente che non sbagliava: gente che non perdeva le cose,
che non lasciava i cassetti in disordine, che non rientrava
tardi la notte. Ma la loro madre filava via libera dopo la
spesa, del resto faceva male la spesa, si faceva imbrogliare
dal macellaio, molte volte anche le davano il resto sbagliato: filava via e non era possibile raggiungerla lí dov'e-
ra, loro in fondo l'ammiravano molto quando filava via:
chi sa com'era quel suo ufficio, non ne parlava spesso:
doveva battere a macchina e scriver lettere in francese e
in inglese: chi sa, forse in questo era abbastanza brava.

Un giorno ch'erano andati a fare una passeggiata con
don Vigliani e con altri ragazzi del ricreatorio,[3] al ritorno
videro la madre in un caffè di periferia. Stava seduta
dentro il caffè, la videro dai vetri, e un uomo era seduto
con lei. La madre aveva posato sul tavolo la sua sciarpa
scozzese e la vecchia borsetta di coccodrillo che conoscevano bene: l'uomo aveva un largo paltò chiaro e dei baffi
castani e parlava con lei sorridendo: la madre aveva un
viso felice, disteso e felice, come non aveva mai a casa.
Guardava l'uomo e si tenevano le mani, e lei non vide i
ragazzi: i ragazzi continuarono a camminare accanto a
don Vigliani che diceva a tutti di far presto perché bisognava prendere il tram: quando furono in tram il ragazzo
piú piccolo si avvicinò al fratello e gli disse – Hai visto
la mamma –, e il fratello disse – No, non l'ho vista –.
Il piú piccolo rise piano e disse: – Ma sì che l'hai vista,
era proprio la mamma e c'era un signore con lei –. Il ragazzo piú grande volse via la testa: era grande, aveva
quasi tredici anni: il fratello minore lo irritava perché
gli faceva pena, non capiva perché ma gli faceva pena,
aveva pena anche di sè e non voleva pensare a quella cosa
che aveva visto, voleva fare come se non avesse visto
nulla.

Non dissero niente alla nonna. Al mattino mentre la
madre si vestiva il ragazzo piccolo disse: – Ieri quando
siamo andati a fare la passeggiata con don Vigliani ti

day: they were people like Granny or like Diomira, large soft imperious bodies of people who didn't make mistakes: people who didn't lose things, who didn't leave their drawers untidy, who didn't come home late at night. But their mother ran off free after the shopping; besides, she was bad at shopping, she got cheated by the butcher and was often given wrong change: she went off and it was impossible to join her where she went, deep down they marvelled at her enormously when they saw her go off: who knows what that office of hers was like, she didn't talk about it much; she had to type and write letters in French and English: who knows, maybe she was pretty good at that.

One day when they were out for a walk with Don Vigliani and with other boys from the youth club, on the way back they saw their mother in a suburban café. She was sitting inside the café; they saw her through the window, and a man was sitting with her. Their mother had laid her tartan scarf on the table and the old crocodile handbag they knew well: the man had a loose light overcoat and a brown moustache and was talking to her and smiling: their mother's face was happy, relaxed and happy, as it never was at home. She was looking at the man and they were holding hands and she didn't see the boys: the boys went on walking beside Don Vigliani who told them all to hurry because they must catch the tram: when they were on the tram the younger boy moved over to his brother and said: 'Did you see Mummy?' and his brother said: 'No, I didn't.' The younger one laughed softly and said: 'Oh yes you did, it was Mummy and there was a man with her.' The older boy turned his head away: he was big, nearly thirteen: his younger brother irritated him because he made him feel sorry for him, he couldn't understand why he felt sorry for him but he was sorry for himself as well and he didn't want to think of what he had seen, he wanted to behave as if he had seen nothing.

They said nothing to Granny. In the morning while their mother was dressing the younger boy said: 'Yesterday when we were out for a walk with Don Vigliani we saw you and

abbiamo vista e c'era anche quel signore con te –. La madre si volse di scatto, aveva un viso cattivo: i pesciolini neri sulla sua fronte guizzarono e si congiunsero insieme. Disse: – Ma non ero io. Figurati. Devo stare in ufficio fino a tardi la sera, lo sai. Si vede che vi siete sbagliati –. Il ragazzo grande disse allora, con una voce stanca e tranquilla: – No, non eri tu. Era una che ti somigliava –. E tutti e due i ragazzi capirono che quel ricordo doveva sparire da loro: e tutti e due respirarono forte per soffiarlo via.

Ma l'uomo dal paltò chiaro venne una volta a casa. Non aveva il paltò perché era estate, aveva degli occhiali azzurri e un vestito di tela chiara, chiese il permesso di levarsi la giacca mentre pranzavano. Il nonno e la nonna erano andati a Milano a incontrarsi con certi parenti e Diomira era andata al suo paese, loro dunque erano soli con la madre. Venne allora quell'uomo. C'era un pranzo abbastanza buono: la madre aveva comprato quasi tutto alla rosticceria: c'era il pollo con le patate fritte e questo viniva dalla rosticceria: la madre aveva fatto la pastasciutta, era buona, solo la salsa s'era un po' bruciata. C'era anche del vino. La madre era nervosa e allegra, voleva dire tante cose insieme: voleva parlare dei ragazzi all'uomo e dell'uomo ai ragazzi. L'uomo si chiamava Max ed era stato in Africa, aveva molte fotografie della Africa e le mostrava: c'era la fotografia d'una sua scimmia, i ragazzi gli chiesero molto di questa scimmia; era cosí intelligente e gli voleva bene e aveva un fare cosí buffo e carino quando voleva avere una caramella. Ma l'aveva lasciata in Africa perché era malata e aveva paura che morisse nel piroscafo. I ragazzi fecero amicizia con questo Max. Lui promise di portarli al cinema una volta. Gli mostrarono i loro libri, non ne avevano molti: lui chiese se avevano letto *Saturnino Farandola* e loro dissero di no e disse che gliel'avrebbe regalato, e poi anche *Robinson delle praterie*[4] perché era molto bello. Dopo pranzo la madre disse loro di andare al ricreatorio a giocare. Avrebbero voluto rimanere ancora con Max. Protestaro-

there was a man with you.' Their mother jerked round, looking nasty: the black fish on her forehead quivered and met. She said: 'But it wasn't me. What an idea. I've got to stay in the office till late in the evening, as you know. Obviously you made a mistake.' The older boy then said, in a tired calm voice: 'No, it wasn't you. It was someone who looked like you.' And both boys realized that the memory must disappear: and they both breathed hard to blow it away.

But the man in the light overcoat once came to the house. He hadn't got his overcoat because it was summer, he wore blue spectacles and a light linen suit, he asked leave to take off his jacket while they had lunch. Granny and Grandpa had gone to Milan to meet some relations and Diomira had gone to her village, so they were alone with their mother. It was then the man came. Lunch was pretty good: their mother had bought nearly everything at the cooked meat shop: there was chicken with chips and this came from the shop: their mother had done the pasta, it was good, only the sauce was a bit burnt. There was wine, too. Their mother was nervous and gay, she wanted to say so much at once: she wanted to talk of the boys to the man and of the man to the boys. The man was called Max and he had been in Africa, he had lots of photographs of Africa and showed them: there was a photograph of a monkey of his, the boys asked him about this monkey a lot; it was so intelligent and so fond of him and had such a funny, pretty way with it when it wanted a sweet. But he had left it in Africa because it was ill and he was afraid it would die on the steamer. The boys became friendly with this Max. He promised to take them to the cinema one day. They showed him their books, they hadn't got many: he asked them if they had read *Saturnino Farandola* and they said no and he said he would give it to them, and *Robinson delle praterie* as well, as it was very fine. After lunch their mother told them to go and play in the recreation ground. They wished they could stay on with Max. They protested a bit but their mother, and

no un poco ma la madre e anche Max dissero che
dovevano andare; e la sera quando ritornarono a casa
non c'era piú Max. La madre preparò in fretta la cena,
caffelatte e insalata di patate: loro erano contenti, volevano parlare dell'Africa e della scimmia, erano straordina-
riamente contenti e non capivano bene perché: e anche
la madre pareva contenta e raccontava delle cose, una
scimmia che aveva visto ballare sull'organetto una volta.
Poi disse loro di coricarsi e disse che sarebbe uscita per un
momentino, non dovevano aver paura, non c'era motivo;
si chinò a baciarli e disse che era inutile raccontare di
Max al nonno e alla nonna perché loro non avevano mai
piacere che si invitasse la gente.

Dunque rimasero soli con la madre per alcuni giorni:
mangiavano delle cose insolite perché la madre non aveva
voglia di cucinare, prosciutto e marmellata e caffelatte e
cose fritte della rosticceria. Poi lavavano i piatti tutti insieme. Ma quando il nonno e la nonna tornarono i ragazzi
si sentirono sollevati: c'era di nuovo la tovaglia sulla ta-
vola a pranzo e i bicchieri e tutto quello che ci voleva:
c'era di nuovo la nonna seduta nella poltrona a dondolo
col suo corpo mansueto e col suo odore: la nonna non
poteva scappar via, era troppo vecchia e troppo grassa,
era bello avere qualcuno che stava in casa e non poteva
mai scappar via.

I ragazzi alla nonna non dissero nulla di Max. Aspettavano il libro di *Saturnino Farandola* e aspettavano che
Max li portasse al cinema e mostrasse altre fotografie
della scimmia. Una volta o due chiesero alla madre
quando sarebbero andati al cinema col signor Max. Ma
la madre rispose dura che il signor Max adesso era par-
tito. Il ragazzo piú piccolo chiese se non era forse andato
in Africa. La madre non rispose nulla. Ma lui pensava che
certo era andato in Africa a ripigliarsi la scimmia.
S'immaginava che un giorno o l'altro venisse a prenderli
a scuola, con un servo negro e con la scimmia in collo.
Ricominciarono le scuole e venne la zia Clementina a
stare un po' da loro; aveva portato un sacco di pere e di

Max too, said they must go; then in the evening when they came home Max was no longer there. Their mother hurriedly prepared the supper, coffee with milk and potato salad: they were happy, they wanted to talk about Africa and the monkey, they were extraordinarily happy and couldn't really understand why: and their mother seemed happy too and told them things, about a monkey she had once seen dancing to a little street organ. And then she told them to go to bed and said she was going out for a minute, they mustn't be scared, there was no reason to be; she bent down to kiss them and told them there was no point in telling Granny and Grandpa about Max because they never liked one inviting people home.

So they stayed on their own with their mother for a few days: they ate unusual things because their mother didn't want to cook, ham and jam and coffee with milk and fried things from the cooked meat shop. Then they washed up together. But when Granny and Grandpa came back the boys felt relieved: the tablecloth was on the dining-room table again, and the glasses and everything there should be: Granny was sitting in her rocking chair again, with her soft body and her smell: Grandma couldn't dash off, she was too old and too fat, it was nice having someone who stayed at home and couldn't ever dash away.

The boys said nothing to Granny about Max. They waited for the book *Saturnino Farandola* and waited for Max to take them to the cinema and show them more photographs of the monkey. Once or twice they asked their mother when they'd be going to the cinema with signor Max. But their mother answered harshly that signor Max had left now. The younger boy asked if he'd gone to Africa. Their mother didn't answer. But he thought he must have gone to Africa to fetch the monkey. He imagined that someday or other he would come and fetch them at school, with a black servant and a monkey in his arms. School began again and Aunt Clementina came to stay with them for a while; she had brought a bag of pears and apples which they put in the

LA MADRE

mele che si mettevano a cuocere in forno col marsala e lo
zucchero. La madre era molto di cattivo umore e litigava
di continuo col nonno. Rientrava tardi la notte e stava
sveglia a fumare. Era molto dimagrita e non mangiava
nulla. Il suo viso si faceva sempre piú piccolo, giallo;
adesso anche si dava il nero alle ciglia, sputava dentro
una scatoletta e con uno spazzolino tirava su il nero lí
dove aveva sputato; metteva moltissima cipria, la nonna
voleva levargliela col fazzoletto e lei scostava via il viso.
Non parlava quasi mai e quando parlava pareva che facesse
fatica, la sua voce veniva su debole. Un giorno tornò a
casa nel pomeriggio verso le sei: era strano, di solito rientrava molto piú tardi: si chiuse a chiave nella stanza da
letto. Il ragazzo piú piccolo venne a bussare perché aveva
bisogno d'un quaderno: la madre rispose da dentro con
una voce arrabbiata, che voleva dormire e la lasciassero
in pace: il ragazzo spiegò timidamente che gli serviva il
quaderno; allora venne ad aprire e aveva la faccia tutta
gonfia e bagnata: il ragazzo capí che stava piangendo,
tornò dalla nonna e disse: – La mamma piange, – e la
nonna e la zia Clementina parlarono a lungo sottovoce
tra loro, parlavano della madre ma non si capiva cosa
dicevano.

Una notte la madre non ritornò a casa. Il nonno venne
molte volte a vedere, scalzo, col cappotto sul pigiama;
venne anche la nonna e i ragazzi dormirono male, sentivano la nonna e il nonno che camminavano per la casa,
aprivano e chiudevano le finestre. I ragazzi avevano
molta paura. Poi al mattino telefonarono dalla questura:
la madre l'avevano trovata morta in un albergo, aveva
preso il veleno, aveva lasciato una lettera: andarono il
nonno e la zia Clementina, la nonna urlava, i ragazzi
furono mandati al piano di sotto da una vecchia signora
che diceva continuamente: – Senza cuore, lasciare due
creature cosí. – La madre la riportarono a casa. I ragazzi
andarono a vederla quando l'ebbero distesa sul letto:
Diomira le aveva messo le scarpe di vernice e l'aveva

oven to cook with marsala and sugar. Their mother was in a very bad temper and quarrelled continually with Grandpa. She came home late and stayed awake smoking. She had got very much thinner and ate nothing. Her face became ever smaller and yellower, she now put black on her eyelashes too, she spat into a little box and picked up the black where she had spat with a brush; she put on masses of powder, Granny tried to wipe it off her face with a handkerchief and she turned her face away. She hardly ever spoke and when she did it seemed an effort, her voice was so weak. One day she came home in the afternoon at about six o'clock: it was strange, usually she came home much later; she locked herself in the bedroom. The younger boy came and knocked because he needed an exercise book: their mother answered angrily from inside that she wanted to sleep and that they were to leave her in peace: the boy explained timidly that he needed the exercise book; then she came to open up and her face was all swollen and wet: the boy realized she was crying, he went back to Granny and said: 'Mummy's crying,' and Granny and Aunt Clementina talked quietly together for a long time, they spoke of their mother but you couldn't make out what they were saying.

One night their mother didn't come home. Grandpa kept coming to see, barefoot, with his overcoat over his pyjamas; Granny came too and the boys slept badly, they could hear Granny and Grandpa walking about the house, opening and shutting the windows. The boys were very frightened. Then in the morning, they rang up from the police station: their mother had been found dead in an hotel, she had taken poison, she had left a letter: Grandpa and Aunt Clementina went along, Granny shrieked, the boys were sent to an old lady on the floor below who said continually: 'Heartless, leaving two babes like this.' Their mother was brought home. The boys went to see her when they had her laid out on the bed: Diomira had dressed her in her patent leather shoes and the red silk dress from the time she was

vestita col vestito di seta rossa di quando s'era sposata:
era piccola, una piccola bambola morta.

Riusciva strano vedere fiori e candele nella solita stanza. Diomira e la zia Clementina e la nonna stavano inginocchiate a pregare: avevan detto che s'era preso il veleno per sbaglio, perché se no il prete non veniva a benedirla, se sapeva che l'aveva fatto apposta. Diomira disse ai ragazzi che la dovevano baciare: si vergognavano terribilmente e la baciarono uno dopo l'altro sulla gota fredda. Poi ci fu il funerale, durò molto, traversarono tutta la città e si sentivano molto stanchi: c'era anche don Vigliani, poi c'erano tanti ragazzi della scuola e del ricreatorio. Faceva freddo, al cimitero tirava un gran vento. Quando tornarono a casa, la nonna si mise a piangere e gridare divanti alla bicicletta nell'andito: perché pareva proprio di vederla quando filava via, col suo corpo libero e la sciarpa che svolazzava nel vento: don Vigliani diceva che adesso era in Paradiso, perché lui forse non sapeva che l'aveva fatto apposta, o lo sapeva e faceva finta di niente: ma i ragazzi non sapevano bene se il Paradiso c'era davvero, perché il nonno diceva di no, e la nonna diceva di sì, e la madre una volta aveva detto che non c'è il Paradiso, con gli angioletti e con la bella musica, ma da morti si va in un posto dove non si sta né bene né male, e dove non si desidera nulla ci si riposa e si sta molto in pace.

I ragazzi andarono in campagna per qualche tempo dalla zia Clementina. Tutti erano molto buoni con loro, e li baciavano e li accarezzavano, e loro avevano molta vergogna. Non parlarono mai della madre fra loro, e neppure del signor Max; nella soffitta della zia Clementina trovarono il libro di *Saturnino Farandola* e lo lessero e lo lessero e trovarono che era bello. Ma il ragazzo piú grande pensava tante volte alla madre, come l'aveva vista quel giorno al caffè, con Max che le teneva le mani e con un viso cosí disteso e felice; pensava allora che forse la madre aveva preso il veleno perché Max era forse tornato in Africa per sempre. I ragazzi giocavano col cane della

married: she was small, a small dead doll.

It was strange to see flowers and candles in the same old room. Diomira and Aunt Clementina and Granny were kneeling and praying: they had said she took the poison by mistake, otherwise the priest wouldn't come and bless her, if he knew she had done it on purpose. Diomira told the boys they must kiss her: they were terribly ashamed and kissed her cold cheek one after the other. Then there was the funeral, it took ages, they crossed the entire town and felt very tired, Don Vigliani was there too and a great many children from school and from the youth club. It was cold, and very windy in the cemetery. When they went home again, Granny started crying and bawling at the sight of the bicycle in the passage: because it was really just like seeing her dashing away, with her free body and her scarf flapping in the wind: Don Vigliani said she was now in heaven, perhaps because he didn't know she had done it on purpose, or he knew and pretended not to: but the boys didn't really know if heaven existed, because Grandpa said no, and Granny said yes, and their mother had once said there was no heaven, with little angels and beautiful music, but that the dead went to a place where they were neither well nor ill, and that where you wish for nothing you rest and are wholly at peace.

The boys went to the country for a time, to Aunt Clementina's. Everyone was very kind to them, and kissed and caressed them, and they were very ashamed. They never spoke together of their mother nor of signor Max either; in the attic at Aunt Clementina's they found the book of *Saturnino Farandola* and they read it over and over and found it very fine. But the older boy often thought of his mother, as he had seen her that day in the café with Max, holding her hands and with such a relaxed, happy face; he thought then that maybe their mother had taken poison because Max had gone back to Africa for good. The boys played with Aunt Clementina's dog, a fine dog called Bubi, and

zia Clementina, un bel cane che si chiamava Bubi, e impararono ad arrampicarsi sugli alberi, perché prima non erano capaci.[6] Andavano anche a fare il bagno nel fiume, ed era bello tornare la sera dalla zia Clementina a fare i cruciverba tutti insieme. I ragazzi erano molto contenti di stare dalla zia Clementina. Poi tornarono a casa dalla nonna e furono molto contenti. La nonna sedeva nella poltrona a dondolo, e voleva pulir loro le orecchie con le sue forcine. La domenica andavano al cimitero, veniva anche Diomira, compravano dei fiori e al ritorno si fermavano al bar a prendere il ponce caldo. Quando erano al cimitero, davanti alla tomba, la nonna pregava e piangeva, ma era molto difficile pensare che le tombe e le croci e il cimitero c'entrassero per qualche cosa con la madre, quella che si faceva imbrogliare dal macellaio e filava via in bicicletta, e fumava e sbagliava le strade e singhiozzava la notte. Il letto era ora molto grande per loro, e avevano un guanciale per uno. Non pensavano spesso alla madre perché faceva un po' male e vergogna pensarci. Si provavano a volte a ricordare com'era, in silenzio ciascuno per conto suo: e si trovavano a mettere insieme sempre piú faticosamente i capelli corti e ricciuti e i pesciolini neri sulla sua fronte e le labbra: metteva molta cipria gialla, questo lo ricordavano bene; a poco a poco ci fu un punto giallo, impossibile riavere la forma delle gote e del viso. Del resto adesso capivano che non l'avevano amata molto, forse anche lei non li amava molto, se li avesse amati non avrebbe preso il veleno, cosí avevano sentito che diceva Diomira e il portinaio e la signora del piano di sotto e tanta altra gente. Gli anni passavano e i ragazzi crescevano e succedevano tante cose e quel viso che non avevano molto amato svaniva per sempre.

they learnt to climb trees, as they couldn't do before. They went bathing in the river, too, and it was nice going back to Aunt Clementina's in the evening and doing crosswords all together. The boys were very happy at Aunt Clementina's. Then they went back to Granny's and were very happy. Granny sat in the rocking chair, and wanted to clean their ears with her hairpins. On Sunday they went to the cemetery, Diomira came too, they bought flowers and on the way back stopped at a bar to have hot punch. When they were in the cemetery, at the grave, Granny prayed and cried, but it was very hard to think that the grave and the crosses and the cemetery had anything to do with their mother, who had been cheated by the butcher and dashed off on her bicycle, and smoked, and took wrong turnings, and sobbed at night. The bed was very big for them now and they had a pillow each. They didn't often think of their mother because it hurt them a little and made them ashamed to think of her. Sometimes they tried to remember how she was, each on his own in silence: and they found it harder and harder to reassemble her short curly hair and the fish on her forehead and her lips: she put on a lot of yellow powder, this they remembered quite well; little by little there was a yellow dot, it was impossible to get the shape of her cheeks and face. Besides, they now realized that they had never loved her much, perhaps she too hadn't loved them much, if she had loved them she wouldn't have taken poison, they had heard Diomira and the porter and the lady on the floor below and so many other people say so. The years went by and the boys grew and so many things happened and that face which they had never loved very much disappeared for ever.

ANGUISH
ALBERTO MORAVIA

Translated by Angus Davidson

L'ANGOSCIA

Lorenzo fermò la macchina e si voltò verso il giovane: «Allora tu vieni su o vuoi restare qui?»

Lo vide alzare le spalle, con espressione di proterva infingardaggine: «E chi ci va su? Manco morto.»[1]

Lorenzo lo guardò un momento, senza parlare. Il volto bello e corrotto, molto bruno, dagli occhi neri e umidi di forma e grandezza femminili, dal naso corto e sensuale, dalle labbra carnose, lustre e tumide, gli ripugnava e ancor piú lo sorprendeva: come avevano fatto i genitori a non accorgersi di niente? Quel volto parlava. Lorenzo disse annoiato: «Lionello, se dovevi prenderla in questo modo, era meglio che non venissi da me.»

«Ma, avvocato,[2] come dovrei prenderla?»

«Ma ti rendi conto che puoi finire in galera?»

Il ragazzo lo guardò, si assestò meglio sui cuscini della macchina, mezzo sdraiato, col capo rovesciato indietro e il collo tondo e forte fuori della maglia estiva, ma non disse niente. Era la sua maniera di rispondere alle domande imbarazzanti. Lorenzo insistette: «Si può sapere almeno perché l'hai fatto?»

Nuovo silenzio. Lo sguardo del ragazzo, filtrato dall'alto in basso, tra le lunghe ciglia, irritava Lorenzo: «Ma allora perché sei venuto da me?»

Questa volta Lionello si decise a parlare, lentamente e con disdegno. «Sono venuto da lei perché ho pensato che lei fosse piú comprensivo. Ma se mi fa queste domande, allora vuol dire che mi sono sbagliato e che ho fatto male.»

«Hai fatto male a far che cosa?»

«A venire da lei.»

Lorenzo saltò fuori dalla macchina e sbatté con forza

134

ANGUISH

Lorenzo stopped the car and turned towards the youth. 'Well then, are you coming up or d'you want to stay here?'

He saw him shrug his shoulders, with an expression of arrogant laziness. 'Who's going up? I'm not, not even dead.'

Lorenzo looked at him for a moment, without speaking. The handsome, depraved face, very dark, with its black, moist eyes of feminine size and shape, its short, sensual nose, its fleshy, glossy, swelling lips, was repugnant to him and, even more, surprised him: how had his parents failed to notice anything? It was a face that spoke. Lorenzo, annoyed, said: 'Lionello, if you're going to take it like this, it would have been better not to come to me.'

'But, *avvocato*, how ought I to take it?'

'D'you realize you may end up in prison?'

The boy looked at him, settled himself back on the cushions of the car, half lying down, his head thrown back and his neck rising round and strong above his summer jersey; but he said nothing. It was his way of answering embarrassing questions. Lorenzo insisted. 'May one at least know why you did it?'

Again silence. The look in the boy's eyes, filtering downwards through his long lashes, irritated Lorenzo. 'Why did you come to me, then?' he asked.

This time Lionello decided to speak, slowly and disdainfully. 'I came to you because I thought you were more understanding. But if you ask me these questions, then it means that I made a mistake and did wrong.'

'Did wrong in doing what?'

'In coming to you.'

Lorenzo jumped out of the car and slammed the door

la portiera: «E va bene, resta qui, io vado di sopra.» Ma nel momento che passava accanto alla macchina, vide il ragazzo fare, con la mano, un languido gesto di richiamo, senza, però, modificare la posizione neghittosa e sdraiata. Si fermò e domandò irritato: «E ora che vuoi?»

«Sigarette.»

«Tieni.» Lorenzo gettò il pacchetto in faccia al ragazzo e poi entrò nell'atrio. Come fu davanti l'ascensore, scorse, con la coda dell'occhio, là di fuori nella strada, una figura femminile avvicinarsi all'automobile e parlare a Lionello. La riconobbe subito, era la sorella, Gigliola. Mentre Lionello aveva la faccia e i modi, non si sapeva bene se coltivati o spontanei, di un teppista delle borgate, Gigliola, dal canto suo, con il suo corpo flessuoso ed eccessivamente ancheggiante, la sua faccia piatta e senza fronte, i suoi occhi troppo grandi e la sua bocca troppo larga, aveva molto del personaggio femminile corrispondente. Lorenzo indugiò apposta presso l'ascensore in modo da permetterle di arrivare. La vide, infatti, giungere finalmente, camminando sui marmi specchianti del vasto atrio, mezza nuda nel vestitino che pareva ricavato da un fazzoletto e che le lasciava scoperte le spalle, le braccia, il sommo del petto e le gambe fin sopra le ginocc..ia. Lorenzo notò che la pettinatura alla moda, in forma di alta cresta ovale, confermava e sottolineava la straordinaria bassezza della fronte, non piú di due dita, e la larghezza e robustezza animalesca della parte inferiore del viso. Gigliola entrò nell'ascensore e domandò a Lorenzo, senza salutarlo: «Ma che ha Lionello? Perché non vuole venir su? E perché si nasconde nella sua macchina?»

Lorenzo entrò a sua volta nell'ascensore e disse, chiudendo le porte: «Lionello sta nei guai.»

«L'ha fatta grossa, eh.»

«Grossissima.»

«Ma che ha fatto?»

hard. 'All right, then, stay here, I'll go up.' But, just as he was walking past the car, he saw the boy make a languid gesture of appeal with his hand, without, however, modifying his listless, lounging position. He stopped and inquired irritably: 'And now what d'you want?'

'Cigarettes.'

'Here you are.' Lorenzo threw the packet into the boy's face and then went into the entrance hall. As he stood in front of the lift he noticed, out of the tail of his eye, a female figure, outside in the street, approach the car and speak to Lionello. He recognized her at once; it was the boy's sister, Gigliola. While Lionello had the face and the manners – whether cultivated or spontaneous, it was impossible to be sure – of a young hooligan from the suburbs, Gigliola, on her side, with her supple body that swayed too much from the hips, her flat, foreheadless face, her eyes that were too large and her mouth that was too wide, had much of the corresponding female type. Lorenzo lingered on purpose beside the lift so as to allow her to come up with him. Finally, indeed, he saw her approach, walking across the shining marble of the spacious hall, half naked in her little dress which looked as though cut out of a handkerchief and which left her shoulders uncovered, as well as her arms, the upper part of her bosom and her legs up to above her knees. Lorenzo noticed that her fashionable hair-style, in the form of a tall oval crest, confirmed and emphasized the extraordinary lowness of her forehead, not more than two fingers high, and the breadth and animal-like robustness of the lower part of her face. Gigliola entered the lift and, without greeting him, asked Lorenzo: 'What's wrong with Lionello? Why won't he come upstairs? And why is he hiding in your car?'

Lorenzo, in turn, entered the lift and said, as he closed the door: 'Lionello is in trouble.'

'He's got himself into a mess, has he?'

'A very bad mess.'

'But what's he done?'

«Brava, se te lo dico, subito dopo lo sa tutta Roma.»

«Ma io tanto l'indovino lo stesso. Lionello e gli altri ragazzi dicevano sempre che volevano fare qualche cosa per rompere la monotonia della vita.» Disse queste parole come citandole a memoria, con una serietà ingenua e ottusa che, quasi suo malgrado, fece sorridere Lorenzo: «Ah dicevano cosí?»

«Si, e dicevano pure che avrebbero fatto qualche cosa per cui tutti i giornali avrebbero parlato di loro. Volevo entrarci anch'io ma non mi vollero. Dicevano che non erano cose da donne.»

L'ascensore si fermò ed essi discesero su un pianerottolo, non meno dell'atrio, lustro di marmi. Lorenzo si voltò verso la ragazza, e l'afferrò per un braccio: «Sta' attenta: se vuoi bene³ a tuo fratello, le cose che adesso mi hai detto, non devi dirle a nessuno.»

«Non dirò niente se lei mi dice quello che ha fatto Lionello. Altrimenti . . .»

Non finí perché Lorenzo l'afferrò per le due braccia esclamando: «Non far la stupida. Tu non devi dire niente e basta.»

La stringeva con forza, la vide guardarlo con espressione nient'affatto offesa e poi dire in tono quasi lusingato: «che maniere»; e al tempo stesso accennare un movimento in avanti, provocante, con il ventre. Allora la lasciò subito e disse in fretta: «Insomma Lionello è meno compromesso degli altri. Se tu non parli, potrà anche cavarsela. E piantala di fare la stupida.»

«Che modi. L'avvocato di famiglia,» motteggiò la ragazza. La porta si aprí e un cameriere in giacca bianca li fece entrare in anticamera.

Gigliola disse: «Arrivederci, avvocato,» e si avviò cantarellando e ballonzolando, nell'ombra di un corridoio. Il cameriere introdusse Lorenzo nel salotto.

La madre di Lionello, Giulia, stava girando per il

'Clever girl. If I told you, the whole of Rome would get to know at once.'

'I think I can make a pretty good guess, all the same. Lionello and the other boys were always saying they wanted to do something to break the monotony of life.' She uttered these words as though quoting them from memory, with an ingenuous, blunt seriousness which made Lorenzo smile almost against his will. 'Ah, they said that, did they?'

'Yes, and they also said they would do something for which all the newspapers would talk about them. I wanted to go in with them but they wouldn't have me. They said such things were not for women.'

The lift came to a stop and they got out on to a landing which, no less than the hall, was glossy with marble. Lorenzo turned towards the girl and took her by the arm. 'Now mind what I say: if you love your brother, the things you've just told me, you mustn't mention to anybody.'

'I won't say anything if you tell me what Lionello has done. Otherwise – '

She did not finish, for Lorenzo seized her by both arms, exclaiming: 'Don't play the fool. You mustn't say anything, and that's that.'

He gripped her tightly and saw her look at him with an expression that was not in the least offended. Then she said, in an almost flattered tone of voice: 'What a way to behave!'; and at the same time she made a slight forward movement, a provoking movement, with her belly. At that, he let go of her immediately and said hurriedly: 'On the whole, Lionello is less compromised than the others. If you don't talk, he may even get away with it. And stop playing the fool.'

'What a way to talk! The family lawyer!' mocked the girl. The door opened and a manservant in a white jacket ushered them into the ante-room.

'Good-bye, *avvocato*,' said Gigliola, and went off, humming and dancing along, into the darkness of a corridor. The manservant showed Lorenzo into the drawing-room.

Lionello's mother, Giulia, was wandering round the room

salotto con un piccolo uomo calvo il quale teneva un
metro in mano. Strinse di sfuggita la mano a Lorenzo,
dicendo: «Mi scusi, debbo discutere un momento di
fodere estive con il tappezziere. Vengo subito.» Lorenzo
si domandò se gli convenisse parlare prima a Giulia che
al marito; e alla fine pensò che poteva essere utile: in
fondo, in quella casa, tutto dipendeva da Giulia. Intanto
si era seduto in una poltrona e la guardava mentre
discuteva con l'artigiano. Era alta, magra, stretta, vestita
di grigio e di nero, con l'eleganza spenta propria a
molte donne molto ricche e molto casalinghe. Nei
capelli bruni pettinati con molta cura, c'era già qualche
filo bianco; gli occhi azzurri, piccoli e profondi, avevano
uno scintillio inquietante; il volto di un ovale perfetto
pareva un po' gonfio, forse a causa della esiguità del naso.

Giulia congedò finalmente il tappezziere, venne a
sedersi accanto a Lorenzo e cominciò a parlargli, al
solito, della famiglia alla quale lei si dedicava instan-
cabilmente e che le dava, secondo le sue stesse parole, un
da fare da morire. Parlava in gran fretta, allacciando
precipitosamente l'una frase all'altra, anche quando il
senso non lo richiedeva, un po' come fumano certi
accaniti fumatori i quali accendono la sigaretta nuova
al mozzicone di quella precedente. Si sarebbe detto
che avesse temuto che Lorenzo l'interrompesse e che
avesse saputo in anticipo che lui doveva dirle qualche
cosa di spiacevole. Più volte Lorenzo tentò di insinuare la
frase che gli stava sulla punta della lingua: «Senta Giulia,
a proposito dei suoi figli, dovrei parlarle di Lionello . . .»;
ma tutte le volte si scontrò in un muro di parole, al
tempo stesso mobile e invalicabile. Stranamente, pensò
Lorenzo, mentre nei discorsi traspariva il compiacimento
di chi ha la coscienza a posto e non ha niente da rim-
proverarsi, la fretta e quasi l'orgasmo con cui lei parlava
parevano indicare una angoscia profonda benché, forse,
inconsapevole. Aveva preso a parlarle delle fodere estive

with a little bald man who held a measure in his hand. She shook Lorenzo's hand in passing, saying: 'Forgive me, I have to discuss the question of summer chair-covers for a moment with the upholsterer. I'll come in a minute.' Lorenzo wondered whether it was advisable for him to speak to Giulia before seeing her husband; in the end he decided that it might be useful: in that house everything depended, fundamentally, on Giulia. Meanwhile he had sat down in an armchair and was watching her as she discussed matters with the tradesman. She was tall, thin, narrow, dressed in grey and black, with the lifeless elegance characteristic of many women who are very rich and very domesticated. In her carefully arranged brown hair there were already a few white threads; her blue eyes, small and deep-set, had in them a disquieting sparkle; her face, of a perfect oval shape, looked slightly swollen, on account perhaps of the smallness of her nose.

Giulia finally dismissed the upholsterer, came and sat down beside Lorenzo and began talking to him, as usual, about her family, to which she devoted herself tirelessly and which gave her, in her own words, worry enough to kill her. She spoke in great haste, linking up one sentence precipitately with another, even when the sense did not require it, rather like one of those frenzied smokers who light a fresh cigarette from the butt of the preceding one. One would have thought she was afraid that Lorenzo might interrupt her, and that she knew in advance that he had something disagreeable to tell her. Several times Lorenzo attempted to insinuate the phrase which lay on the tip of his tongue: 'Listen, Giulia; on the subject of your children, I must speak to you about Lionello . . .'; but each time he came up against a wall of words that was at the same time both mobile and impassable. Strangely, thought Lorenzo, whereas in her conversation there was apparent the complacency of one who has a conscience at rest and nothing to reproach herself with, the haste, the frenzy almost, with which she talked seemed to indicate a profound, though perhaps unconscious, anguish. She had started by talking about the

per i mobili; dalle fodere era passata alla villeggiatura al mare e ai monti; dalla villeggiatura si era estesa alla moda degli yachts o, come lei li chiamava, delle barche; dalle barche era slittata sui suoi due figli che per lei erano «i miei bambini», e che appunto erano stati invitati ambedue su una di queste barche; adesso, senza alcun nesso e alcuna interruzione, si era messa a descrivere in tutti i piú minuti particolari una festicciola che Gigliola e Lionello avevano offerto sere prima ai loro amici sulle terrazze della casa: «Hanno fatto anche dei numeri di varietà. Ma ci hanno cacciato via, Federico e me, dicendo: «'Sconsigliabile per adulti. Soltanto per i minori di diciott'anni.' Spiritoso, no?»

La porta si aprí e Federico, il marito, entrò lentamente, con il passo affaticato di chi esca da una lunga, forzata immobilità. Era alto, atletico, ma con le spalle un po' curve; il volto dai lineamenti belli e simmetrici appariva, torno torno gli occhi azzurri e la bocca ancora giovanile, tutto segnato da sottili rughe; la fronte sembrava a prima vista ampia e luminosa, ma ad uno sguardo piú attento ci si accorgeva che era semplicemente calva. Al contrario di Giulia che non sapeva frenare la propria parlantina, Federico, come Lorenzo sapeva, si frenava anche troppo, riducendo la conversazione ad un seguito di mezze frasi e di scosse del capo nelle quali sembrava trasparire un'angoscia in fondo non molto diversa da quella della moglie. Federico si avvicinò a Lorenzo e, come ostentando di ignorare la moglie, lo salutò con una cordialità che parve costargli uno sforzo penoso. Lorenzo lo guardò e capí che l'amico doveva aver passato, al solito, una brutta notte: soffriva d'insonnia e, come si esprimeva lui stesso, aveva il sistema nervoso a pezzi. Federico disse brevemente, con voce sommessa: «Andiamo sulla terrazza, vuoi?»

Uscirono sulla vasta terrazza che, in realtà, era un vero giardino pensile sospeso davanti al panorama della città. Faceva caldo, il sole estivo arroventava l'ammattonato, tra le brevi ombre delle piante in cassetta.

summer covers for the furniture; from the covers she had gone on to holidays at the seaside and in the mountains; from holidays she had enlarged upon the fashion for yachts, or, as she called them, boats; from boats she had slipped to the subject of her two children, who for her were 'my babies', and who had actually both been invited on to one of these boats; and now, without any connexion or any interruption, she had begun describing, in all its minutest details, a small party which Gigliola and Lionello had given, some evenings before, for their friends, on the roof terrace of the house: 'They even did variety turns. But they turned us out, Federico and me, saying: "Not suitable for adults. Only for minors of eighteen years old." Witty, wasn't it?'

The door opened and Federico, the husband, came in slowly, with the exhausted step of one who is emerging from a long, forced immobility. He was tall, athletic, but with slightly bent shoulders; his face, with its handsome, symmetrical features, could be seen to be closely marked, all round the blue eyes and the still youthful mouth, with fine wrinkles; his brow, at first sight, appeared ample and luminous, but if you looked more carefully you became aware that it was simply bald. Unlike Giulia who was unable to restrain her own chatter, Federico, as Lorenzo knew, restrained himself all too much, reducing conversation to a series of half-sentences and head-shakings that seemed to betray an anguish which, fundamentally, was not very different from that of his wife. Federico went up to Lorenzo and, as though making a show of ignoring his wife, greeted him with a cordiality that appeared to cost him a painful effort. Lorenzo looked at him and realized that his friend must have passed, as usual, a bad night: he suffered from insomnia and, as he himself expressed it, his nervous system was all to bits. Federico said briefly, in a subdued voice: 'Let's go on the terrace, shall we?'

They went out on to the spacious terrace which was, in truth, a real roof garden poised in front of the panorama of the city. It was hot, and the summer sun scorched the brick paving between the brief shadows of shrubs in boxes.

L'ANGOSCIA

Federico andò verso un angolo del parapetto dal quale
si aveva una vista sul Tevere e su Monte Mario.
Camminava a passi lunghi e muoveva il capo di qua e di
là, a scatti, come chi si senta soffocare e cerchi invano
l'aria. Lorenzo disse, appena furono abbastanza lontani
dal salotto: «Senti, debbo parlarti.»

Federico adesso guardava in giú, pareva che osservasse
proprio la macchina di Lorenzo, ferma presso il marciapiede, piccola e solitaria nel mezzo di un grande
spazio grigio di asfalto. Disse voltandosi: «Parlare a me?
Mi dispiace ma stamani non è possibile.»

Lorenzo spalancò gli occhi meravigliato: «Non è
possibile? E perché?»

Vide Federico contrarre tutto il viso come per una
fitta o altro dolore improvviso. Quindi rispose: «È
impossibile. Non ho la mente abbastanza calma. Non ho
chiuso occhio durante tutta la notte, nonostante i sonni-
feri e, insomma, non mi sento bene.» Disse ancora altre
cose dello stesso genere; e cosí il volto tirato e contratto
come il tono tutto a sbalzi e a scatti, erano quelli di un
uomo che soffra davvero. Questa sofferenza fece pensare
a Lorenzo che, forse, non sarebbe stato prudente parlargli del figlio. Insistette, tuttavia: «Guarda che si tratta
di una cosa che non può essere differita.»

Federico lanciò di nuovo una occhiata alla macchina,
giú, nella strada, nella quale Lionello stava aspettando;
e rispose: «Non ci sono cose che non possono essere
rimandate. Sembrano sempre tanto urgenti e poi ... Te
ne prego, torna domani, magari domani mattina, avrò
dormito, potremo parlare con calma.»

«Ma è una cosa veramente importante.»

«Proprio perché è importante, non voglio saperla. Non
potrei occuparmi adesso di una cosa importante.»

«Allora proprio non vuoi?»

«Ti prego di non insistere.»

Aveva messo una mano sulla spalla di Lorenzo e,
senza parere, lo spingeva attraverso la terrazza, verso il

Federico went towards a corner of the parapet from which one had a view over the Tiber and over Monte Mario. He walked with long steps and moved his head this way and that, jerkily, like a man who feels himself suffocating and seeks in vain for air. As soon as they were far enough away from the drawing-room, Lorenzo said: 'Listen, I must speak to you.'

Federico was now looking down; he seemed to be staring straight at Lorenzo's car standing beside the pavement, small and solitary in the middle of a big, grey space of asphalt. Turning, he said: 'Speak to me? I'm sorry, but this morning it's not possible.'

Lorenzo opened his eyes wide in surprise: 'It's not possible? And why?'

He saw Federico's whole face contract, as if with cramp or some other sudden pain. Then Federico answered: 'It's impossible. My mind is not calm enough. I haven't closed an eye all night in spite of sleeping-draughts, and, in short, I don't feel well.' He said yet other things of the same kind; and both the drawn, shrunken face and the tone of voice, all spasmodic and jerky, were those of a man who is really suffering. This suffering made Lorenzo think that, perhaps, it would not be prudent to speak to him of his son. He persisted, nevertheless: 'Mind you, it's a question of something that cannot be put off.'

Federico again cast a glance at the car down in the street, in which Lionello was waiting; and he replied: 'There are no things that cannot be postponed. They seem always so urgent and then ... I beg you, come back tomorrow, come tomorrow morning, even; I shall have slept, we shall be able to talk calmly.'

'But it's a thing that is really important.'

'Just because it's important, I don't wish to know it. I couldn't occupy myself now with an important thing.'

'Then you really don't want to?'

'Please don't insist.'

He had put his hand on Lorenzo's shoulder and, imperceptibly, was pushing him across the terrace, towards the

salotto. Lorenzo aveva notato che ogni volta che parlava, Federico contraeva il volto come per uno spasimo e decise alla fine, in cuor suo, di non dirgli niente. Avrebbe fatto quel che poteva per Lionello; Giulia e Federico i quali, ciascuno a modo suo, non volevano saper niente, avrebbero appreso le malefatte del figlio dai giornali oppure non le avrebbero apprese affatto. Declinò un blando invito a colazione di Federico, lo salutò, poi andò a stringere la mano a Giulia e passò nell'anticamera.

Come se l'avesse aspettato, ecco, tosto, sorgere dall'ombra Gigliola: «Beh, ha parlato con papà e mammà?»

«No, e, anzi, ti prego di non dir loro niente.»

«Ma chi parla? Però lei dovrebbe convincersene.»

«Di che cosa?»

«Che la sola persona a cui si possa dir tutto in questa casa, sono io.»

«Forse hai ragione.» Lorenzo chiuse le porte dell'ascensore. La cabina cominciò a discendere.

drawing-room. Lorenzo had noticed that, each time he spoke, Federico's face was contracted by a sort of spasm, and in the end he decided, secretly, not to tell him anything. He would do what he could for Lionello; Giulia and Federico who, each in their own way, did not wish to know anything, would learn their son's misdeeds from the newspapers, or would not learn them at all. He declined a bland invitation to lunch from Federico, said good-bye to him, then went and shook Giulia's hand and passed on into the ante-room.

As though she had been waiting for him, there was Gigliola, emerging from the shadows. 'Well,' she said, 'did you speak to Papa and Mamma?'

'No; and, in fact, please don't tell them anything.'

'But who's saying anything? However, you ought to be convinced.'

'Of what?'

'That the only person to whom one can tell everything, in this house, is myself.'

'Perhaps you're right.' Lorenzo closed the doors of the lift. The cage started on its way down.

FOOTSTEPS IN THE SNOW
MARIO SOLDATI

Translated by Gwyn Morris

I PASSI SULLA NEVE

È una goccia, che fa traboccare il vaso.[1] Poco prima
dell'ora di colazione, era tornato in albergo, era salito
in camera. Sua moglie era nel bagno, si stava pettinando:
e non s'era chiusa dentro come d'abitudine. Lui, perciò,
credeva di poter entrare. Ma lei gridò con odio, sí, con
vero e proprio odio:
   «Vuoi chiudere per piacere?!»
   Chiuse, uscí dalla camera, uscí dall'albergo.
   Nevicava sempre.

   Nell'antico ristorante, tutto ori specchi e vetri di-
pinti, mentre faceva colazione, guardava la neve cadere
contro lo sfondo bruno rossastro di Palazzo Carignano.
La neve, posata sui cornicioni barocchi, sulle modana-
ture delle finestre, sul gioco degli sguinci e delle decora-
zioni, ripeteva, ritrovava fatalmente ed esattamente i
tratti leggeri della penna del Guarini,[2] quando, nei
primi rapidi abbozzi, aveva immaginato la facciata del
palazzo. Cosí, Gioberti,[3] al centro della piazza, era
segnato dalla neve soltanto sulle spalle e sulle braccia,
sulle pieghe della redingote, intorno al capo: non pareva
piú un monumento, ma l'impressione di un monumento,
schizzata da un De Pisis[4] con poche pennellate di biacca:
diventava bello anche se non lo era.
   La neve semplificava tutto, come un grande dise-
gnatore.
   Pensò a suo padre, il quale, quando litigava con la
mamma, andava a colazione fuori: e sempre, o quasi sempre, in quello stesso ristorante, dove lui era in quel momento per ragioni analoghe, e che al tempo di suo padre
era identico, in ogni particolare, a oggi e a centotrenta
anni prima. Centotrenta piú quaranta: centosettanta!

FOOTSTEPS IN THE SNOW

It was the last straw that broke the camel's back. Just before lunchtime he had come back to the hotel and gone up to his room. His wife was in the bathroom, combing her hair – she had not locked herself in as she usually did. And so he thought it was all right to go in. But she shouted at him with hate, yes, real hate in her voice:

'Do you mind closing the door please?'

He closed the door, went out of the room, left the hotel. It was still snowing.

While he lunched in the old restaurant with all its gilt decoration, mirrors, and stained glass, he gazed out at the snow falling against the dark russet background of Palazzo Carignano. The snow, lying on the baroque cornices, the window mouldings, the pattern of oblique lines and ornaments, repeated, retraced inevitably and precisely the light strokes of Guarini's pen when in his first rapid sketches he pictured the façade of the palace. Similarly, Gioberti, in the centre of the square, was limned in snow only on the shoulders, and arms, the folds of his frock-coat, around his head. It seemed no longer a monument but an impression of a monument dashed off by a De Pisis with a few brush-strokes of white paint. It appeared beautiful even though it wasn't.

The snow simplified everything like a great designer.

He thought of his father who, whenever he quarrelled with his mother, lunched out – always or nearly always in that same restaurant where he was now for like reasons and which in his father's time looked exactly the same in every detail as it was today and had been 130 years before. 130 plus 40 = 170!

Pensò alla vita di suo padre, e pensò alla propria, così diversa e, in un certo senso, così simile. Non esisteva, dunque, una donna in compagnia della quale la vita fosse almeno tollerabile?

Pensò, una dopo l'altra, a tutte le donne che avevano preceduto sua moglie. Cercò di essere oggettivo. Una dopo l'altra, le scartò. Non erano migliori di sua moglie. Erano uguali. La differenza, la leggera preferenza che era tentato di accordare alle altre, consisteva soltanto nel fatto che le altre non le aveva sposate, e lei invece sí. Se avesse sposato una qualunque delle altre, sarebbe immediatamente diventata, ne era sicuro, altrettanto fastidiosa.

Tanto valeva, si disse con un grande sospiro, non perdere tempo e fermarsi alla prima. Ma chi era la prima?

Proprio la prima, trovandosi vicino alla quale gli era passata per il cervello quest'idea assurda ed inevitabile del matrimonio?

Fu una lunga *rêverie*, lunga, lenta, incerta, che affondava nelle lontane stagioni perdute, fino ai tempi dell'adolescenza. E, intanto, i suoi occhi, quasi per conto loro, contemplavano affascinati, in un dolce torpido insulso gioco ottico, la neve che, contro lo scuro Palazzo Carignano, scendeva con ritmo lento e sempre uguale, i fiocchi fitti seguendo però tragitti sempre diversi e formando sempre diverse figure: grandi arabeschi, labili, composti e scomposti prima che si potessero individuare.

Una lunga *rêverie*. Non era possibile ricordarle tutte. Troppo tempo era passato. Ma la prima? La prima?

La prima, senza dubbio alcuno, era stata Lina.
Un po' piú vecchia di lui, forse. Bionda, alta, forte ma insieme rosea, morbida, scattante, spregiudicata, intelligente e tenerissima. Torinese anche lei. Impiegata in una banca.

Avevano flirtato, nelle nostre campagne uno direbbe

He thought of his father's life and then he thought of his own, so different and yet in a way so similar. Wasn't there a woman in existence then with whom life might at least be tolerable?

One after the other, he thought of all the women who had preceded his wife. He tried to be objective. One after the other, he dismissed them. They were no better than his wife. They were just the same. The only difference, the slight preference that he was tempted to allow the others lay merely in the fact that he had not married *them* whereas he had married *her*. If he had married any one of the others she would have immediately become quite as tiresome – he was sure of it.

He might as well have saved time and stopped at the first – he told himself, heaving a deep sigh. But who was the first?

Who was the very first he had been with when this absurd and inevitable idea of marriage flashed through his mind?

It was a long reverie, long, slow, uncertain, delving back into the distant, forgotten past, back to his adolescent days. And meanwhile his eyes, almost independently and as if indulging in some pleasant, lethargic and silly optical exercise, stared fascinated at the snow which was falling gently and steadily against the dark backdrop of Palazzo Carignano, the dense flakes, however, following ever-changing courses and taking ever-changing shapes – great fleeting arabesques forming and disintegrating before the eye could catch them.

A long reverie. It was impossible to remember them all. Too many years had passed. But the first? Who was the first?

The first, without any doubt, had been Lina.

A little bit older than him, perhaps. Blonde, tall, strong but at the same time rosy, soft-skinned, vital, open-minded, intelligent and most tender. A Turin girl, too. A bank-clerk.

They had carried on a flirtation – our countryfolk would

«si erano parlati», un'intera primavera, da marzo a giugno o a luglio, non di piú. Tutto andava benissimo. Lui era stato felice. Piú felice che con qualunque altra donna, dopo, nella vita. Averlo saputo! Averlo potuto sospettare! Ma Lina era stata una felicità improvvisa, completa, gratuita ... Perché mai questa grazia non si sarebbe dovuta ripetere almeno un'altra volta? Aveva tutta la vita davanti a sé! E cosí, l'aveva lasciata.

Era stato lui, anche su questo non c'era dubbio, era stato lui, e non lei, a troncare. E perché?

Per niente. Cosí. Veniva l'estate. C'era di mezzo la villeggiatura⁵: un buon pretesto. Lui, borghese; lei, invece, lavorava. Ma non era per questo che aveva troncato. Aveva troncato soltanto perché aveva vent'anni: non ancora laureato, e nessun impiego in vista: com'era possibile pensare seriamente a un matrimonio?

Eppure, ci aveva pensato: una notte, nel parco di una vecchia villa, allora lontana qualche chilometro, oggi raggiunta dalla periferia della città.

Abbracciando Lina, aveva avuto una sensazione completamente diversa da quella provata con tutte le altre: del resto, fino allora, erano state poche.

Seduti sull'erba, nel profumo di una grande magnolia, in una oscurità quasi completa, lui però le vedeva le labbra rosse, i denti forti e bianchissimi, soprattutto i grandi occhi celesti. Era la prima vera donna della sua vita. Quell'essere, cosí simile al suo stesso essere, e tuttavia cosí profondamente diverso. Quella creatura, che stringeva, con la quale si confondeva, obbedendo in modo naturale e misterioso all'istinto piú bello e piú alto. Per il semplice fatto che non abbracciava piú se stesso ma un'altra persona, gli sembrava di abbracciare l'infinito.

Nel parco della vecchia villa, in quella notte di maggio, ebbe l'infinito contro di sé, sotto le sue labbra, tra le sue mani.

Perché dunque lasciarselo sfuggire?

Perché non vivere insieme, sempre, fino alla morte?

say 'they had spoken to each other' – all spring, from March to June or July, no longer. Everything was fine. He had been happy. Happier than with any other woman later on in life. If only he had known! If only he had even suspected! But Lina had been sudden, complete, gratuitous happiness. . . . Why couldn't this boon be repeated at least once more? He had his whole life before him! And so he had left her.

It had been he – there was no doubt about this, either – he and not she had been the one to break it off. But why?

For nothing at all. Just like that. Summer was coming. Holidays were in the air – a good excuse. He, middle class, she, on the other hand, a working girl. But that was not why he had broken it off. He had broken it off simply because he was twenty, still without a degree and no job in sight – how could he possibly think seriously of marriage?

Yet he had thought of it – when one night in the park of an old villa, then a few kilometres outside the city, today overtaken by a suburb.

Embracing Lina, he had felt a completely different sensation from what he had experienced with all the others. Anyway until then they had been few.

Sitting on the grass, amid the scent of a great magnolia, in almost total darkness, he could still see her red lips, her strong, gleaming white teeth and above all her big, blue eyes. She was the first real woman in his life. A being, so similar to himself and yet so profoundly different. The creature he was holding close, melting into one with her, obeying in a natural yet mysterious way the finest and highest instinct. Due to the simple fact that he was no longer embracing himself but another person, he seemed to be embracing the infinite.

In the grounds of the old villa, that May night, he clasped the infinite tightly to him, beneath his lips, in his hands.

Then why let it slip away? Why not live together, always, till death did them part?

Perché non sposare Lina?

E ci aveva pensato, sí, ci aveva pensato. Ma subito, o quasi subito, aveva allontanato da sé l'idea, come una follia.

Egli sa bene, adesso, a trent'anni di distanza, che forse sarebbe stata la saggezza: o per lo meno una follia non piú grave di quella che poi finí per commettere. Tanto valeva!

Con queste riflessioni, aveva fatto tardi. Dopo la colazione, era rimasto immobile, a guardare la neve ... Quanto tempo? Lo riscosse la voce timida di un cameriere che presentava il conto. La grande sala dorata è scintillante era completamente vuota. Là in fondo, in due signori con pastrano e cappello, riconobbe il padrone e il cameriere piú anziano: evidentemente, aspettavano che lui uscisse per andarsene anche loro.

Guardò l'ora. Erano quasi le cinque. Ecco perché la facciata di Palazzo Carignano non era piú rossastra, ma nera. La notte era vicina. Pagò, e uscí.

Passeggiò sotto i portici senza proporsi una meta.[6] Quando si sarebbe sentito stanco, sarebbe entrato in un caffè: ecco tutto. Ma tornare in albergo, rivedere sua moglie, no, non ancora.

Passeggiò sotto i portici, disperato e felice allo stesso tempo. Fuori, seguitava a nevicare. Si ricordò di aver letto nella guida del Touring che Torino ha quattordici chilometri di portici: quale altra città, in tutto il mondo, offre una comodità cosí civile? Forse Bologna? Padova? Ma non sono alti, ariosi, moderni come questi!

Finalmente, cammina e cammina,[7] era notte ormai da qualche tempo, si ritrovò a quell'angolo di corso Vinzaglio e corso Vittorio, che gli era sempre parso, fino dall'infanzia, il termine estremo di Torino borghese e ottocentesca: quell'angolo, appunto,[8] fino dove si spingevano, incontrandosi per non piú proseguire, i portici dei due corsi, dopo quattordici chilometri impiegati ad

Why not marry Lina?

And he thought about it, yes, he had thought about it. But at once, or almost at once, he had dismissed the idea as sheer folly.

Now, thirty years later, he knew that it might have been the wise thing to do – or at least an act of folly no greater than the one he eventually committed.

It would really have been just as well!

With all these reflections it was getting late. After lunch he had sat motionless looking out at the snow. For how long? He was roused by the timid voice of a waiter presenting the bill. The great glittering gold dining-room was completely empty. There at the other end he recognized two gentlemen in overcoats and hats as the owner and the senior waiter – they were obviously waiting for him to go before leaving themselves.

He looked at the time. It was almost five o'clock. So that was why the façade of Palazzo Carignano was no longer reddish but black. Night was near. He paid up and went out.

He strolled aimlessly along under the arcades. When he felt tired he would turn into a café – that was it. But to go back to the hotel and see his wife again – no, not yet.

He strolled under the arcades, desperate yet happy at the same time. Outside, it was still snowing. He remembered reading in a Touring Club guide that Turin has fourteen kilometres of arcades. What other town in the world can offer such a civilized amenity? Bologna, maybe? Padua? But they are not tall, airy and modern like these!

So he walked on and on and it had been dark for some time when he finally found himself at the corner of Corso Vinzaglio and Corso Vittorio which from his childhood days had always seemed to him the boundary of nineteenth-century bourgeois Turin. That corner, to be exact, where the arcades of the two main streets meet after a journey of fourteen kilometres across the city and up the gentle slope

attraversare la città e a risalirne, dalle rive del Po, il lento declivio su cui era costruita. Oltre quell'angolo era l'ultimo tratto, squallido perché senza portici, di corso Vittorio: erano le Carceri, Borgo San Paolo, gli operai, le fabbriche, l'empio futuro.

Sorrise a quel vecchio pensiero. Il futuro è sempre empio. Lo è per costituzione. Ora, dopo tanti anni, non sentiva più quel distacco fra la città borghese e la città operaia, tra l'ottocento e il novecento. Il vecchio angolo di corso Vinzaglio e corso Vittorio, quasi molo che si protendeva in un mare e nella notte verso il futuro, non era più un molo, non era più un luogo estremo. Il mare, davanti, era diventato terra. Il futuro era diventato presente. E Torino borghese si lasciava abbracciare volentieri da Torino operaia, sua gloria, sua ricchezza e sua difesa.

Comunque, per chi, borghese od operaio, in una notte d'inverno e di neve come quella, camminasse sotto i portici senza meta, cercando sollievo a qualche pena intima, l'angolo di corso Vinzaglio e corso Vittorio era ancora un punto dove veniva naturale di fermarsi.

Quante volte, proprio lí, durante la lontana unica primavera del loro amore, si era fermato la notte con Lina, per poi *rebrousser chemin*![9]

Vide che, lungo il marciapiede, proprio in quell'angolo, c'era, al posteggio, un taxi.

Tornare in albergo? Affrontare la belva?[10]

Sentí stringersi il cuore.

Ma che fare, allora?

Nella lunga marcia sotto i portici, tra il disordine dei ricordi e delle fantasticherie, che parevano scendere e fluire danzando e intrecciandosi come la neve, gli era tornata con insistenza un'immagine preferita, un'immagine dolce, bella, consolatrice: il parco della vecchia villa, la notte di maggio, il volto di Lina sotto i suoi baci.

«Taxi!» gridò con improvvisa decisione. E, salito sul taxi, diceva allo *chauffeur* il nome di quello che tanti anni

on which it is built from the banks of the Po. Beyond the corner was the last stretch of Corso Vittorio, dreary for lack of arcades – here were the Prison, Borgo San Paolo, workers, factories, the cruel future.

He smiled at that old idea. The future is always cruel. It is by nature. Now, after so many years, he no longer felt that gulf between the bourgeois and the working-class city, the nineteenth and the twentieth century. That old corner of Corso Vinzaglio and Corso Vittorio stretching like a jetty out into the sea, the night and the future was no longer a jetty, no longer the farthest limit. The sea, facing him, had become dry land. The future had become the present. And bourgeois Turin willingly accepted the embraces of working-class Turin, her glory, riches and defence.

But, for anyone, bourgeois or working class, on a snowy winter's night like that, strolling aimlessly along the arcades, trying to ease some private grief, the corner of Corso Vinzaglio and Corso Vittorio was still a natural spot to pause.

How often during that one far-off spring of their love, had he stopped right there at night with Lina, before turning to *rebrousser chemin*!

Just at the corner he saw that a taxi was parked in the rank by the pavement.

Should he go back to the hotel? And face that bitch?

He felt a tightening round his heart.

But what was he to do then?

During the long walk through the arcades, in the confusion of memories and daydreams that seemed to fall and flow, dancing and intertwining like snowflakes, a favourite image returned persistently, a sweet, lovely, consoling image: the park at the old villa, that night in May, Lina's face beneath his kisses.

'Taxi' – he called with sudden resolve. And, climbing in, he told the driver the name of what so many years before

fa era un villaggio separato dalla città, ed ora un piccolo centro della periferia.

Quando arrivò, era cessato di nevicare. Lasciò il taxi sulla piazza del paese, ancora intatta con le sue case basse dai grandi portali e dalle grosse mura a sperone: uno contro l'altro, vecchi palazzotti rustici e vecchi cascinali. Ma già, oltre i tetti carichi di neve, a non piú di duecento metri dalla parte di Torino, si vedevano altissimi, geometrici, tutti quadrettati in mille finestre luminose e balconcini, i primi palazzi condominiali, case a riscatto,[11] falansteri[12] di operai e di impiegati.

C'era un caffè ancora aperto. Offrì da bere allo *chauffeur*, e lo pregò di aspettare lí. Non avrebbe fatto tardi.

La villa era a pochi passi: duecento metri, appena fuori dalla piazza. Ricordò. Il cancello appariva, improvviso, in un vicolo dell'antico abitato. A partire da quel punto, il vicolo diventava una strada di campagna, che scendeva verso la non lontana Dora, e che da un lato era fiancheggiata, per un lungo tratto, appunto dal muro di cinta della villa. Si ricordava di un pilone, pochi passi dopo il cancello, di un pilone o di una cappelletta votiva, quasi addossata al muro: e di una breccia nel muro, riempita da un grosso cespuglio e comunque nascosta dalla cappelletta. Il parco era molto grande; la villa, settecentesca, e solitamente disabitata, se non d'autunno, per la villeggiatura.

Forse tutto, oggi, era cambiato. Forse la breccia non c'era piú. Tanti anni! Non importa, aveva bisogno, se non altro, di rivedere quel vecchio muro che aveva circondato il momento (cosí almeno gli sembrava oggi) il momento piú vicino alla verità di tutta la sua vita ... Alla verità o alla felicità? Tutte e due. Le confondeva.

Naturalmente, non fu cosí semplice. Soltanto attraversare la piazza, percorrere il vicolo, e giungere fino al cancello: fu una piccola impresa. Affondava nella

had been a village separated from the city and was now a small suburb.

When he arrived, it had stopped snowing. He left the taxi in the square of the village, still unchanged with its low houses and their large doorways and thick buttressed walls: old country houses and farm cottages huddling together. But already, beyond the snow-laden roofs, and no more than two hundred metres in the direction of Turin, there were to be seen towering, geometrical, chequered by a thousand lighted windows and balconies, the first joint-owned buildings, houses under mortgage, workers' and clerks' ugly blocks of flats.

There was a café still open. He offered the driver a drink and asked him to wait there. He would not be long.

The villa was only a few steps away: two hundred metres, just off the square. He remembered. The gate suddenly appeared in a lane of the old village. From there on, the lane became a country road sloping down to the near-by river Dora and flanked on one side for some distance by the boundary wall of the villa. He recalled a holy-water stoup a few metres past the gate, a holy-water stoup or a votive shrine almost against the wall: and a gap in the wall blocked by a large thicket and hidden, in any case, by the shrine. The park was very big; the villa, eighteenth-century and usually unoccupied except in autumn for the holiday season.

Perhaps today everything had changed. Perhaps the gap was no longer there. So many years! No matter, if nothing else he had to see that old wall again which – at least so it seemed today – had embraced the nearest moment to truth in his whole life . . . To truth or to happiness? Both. He confused the two.

Naturally, it was not so easy. Simply crossing the square, and following the lane as far as the gate – it was quite a little undertaking. He sank up to his calves in the soft,

neve fresca e molle fino ai polpacci, non aveva scarpe adatte. Il vicolo era deserto e semibuio. Vecchie lampadine coi piatti smaltati brillavano come gemme nella notte fredda e pura, ma a grande distanza l'una dall'altra, agli angoli delle case. Se non fosse stato per le musiche, i canti, le risate, le berciate e gli applausi che venivano dai televisori [delle case lungo le quali stava camminando, avrebbe pensato di attraversare un paese abbandonato. Erano voci e suoni, o per lo spessore delle mura, o per la neve alta che copriva tutto, stranamente soffocati, come ovattati.

Presto dileguarono. Non udí piú che il proprio respiro affannoso, e il leggero tonfo di ogni suo passo, quando posava il piede nella neve, alternato allo sfrigolío di quella che ricadeva attorno, quando lo rialzava.

Ecco il cancello. Aveva alle spalle il paese e la città. Davanti, soltanto la villa e la campagna. Se si fermava un momento, e se tratteneva il respiro, lo capiva anche dal silenzio. E in quel silenzio, ormai quasi assoluto, appena riprendeva a camminare il rumore dei propri passi nella neve gli pareva un frastuono.

La cappelletta era lí. Vecchia, scrostata, malandata. Ora, pareva strano che avessero riparato la breccia. Ma, e se lo avevano fatto?

Si inerpicò a fatica sulla proda. Saliva sulla neve: e la neve, smottando a blocchi, lo riportava giú. Ci riuscí, finalmente, mettendosi i guanti ed afferrandosi a una cornice sgretolata, che separava la base della cappelletta dalla vera e propria edicola con l'immagine della Madonna, o di un Santo: c'era la grata, nessun lume dentro: non poté vedere, e non si ricordava.

La neve aveva ricoperto, e confuso in una massa sola, cespuglio e muro. Per accorgersi di una breccia, bisognava saperne l'esistenza.

No, non era stata riparata: e tutta quella neve, ricoprendola, rendeva piú facile il passaggio.

fresh snow as he was not wearing suitable shoes. The lane was deserted and dim. Old lamps with enamelled shades, widely spaced out at the corners of the houses, shone like gems in the cold, pure night air. If it had not been for the music, songs, laughter, bawling and applause coming from the television sets in the houses as he passed by, he might have been walking through a forsaken village. The voices and sounds, either because of the thickness of the walls or the deep snow that covered everything, were strangely muffled as if swathed in cotton-wool.

Soon they died away. All he could hear was his own heavy breathing and the light crunch of each step as he planted his foot in the snow, followed by a splutter as it dropped about when he raised his foot again.

There was the gate. Behind him lay the village and the city. Facing, just the villa and the open countryside. If he paused a moment and held his breath, he could sense it from the silence. And in that silence, now almost absolute, as soon as he set off again, the sound of his footsteps in the snow seemed deafening.

The shrine was there. Old, peeling, dilapidated. Now it seemed unlikely that they would have bothered to repair the gap. But suppose they had?

He struggled up the bank. Up over the snow: and the snow, sliding away in lumps, carried him down again. By putting on his gloves and grasping a crumbling cornice which separated the base of the shrine from the actual niche containing the figure of the Madonna or Saint, he finally made it: there was the grating but no light burning inside; he couldn't see or remember.

The snow had covered in a single mass both thicket and wall. To discover a gap you had to know of its existence.

No, it had not been repaired: and all that snow, by covering it, made it easier to get across.

Quando fu in un viale del parco, si fermò, col cuore che gli batteva, e ascoltò di nuovo il silenzio: ma questa volta a lungo, a lungo, e come in profondità.

L'aria era ferma, tersa e gelida. Vicino, gli unici rumori erano, a quando a quando, gli scricchiolii dei rami che si spezzavano sotto il peso della nuova neve, e i tonfi soffocati che seguivano: e, chissà perché, tonfi, scricchiolii, avevano qualcosa di vivo e di sofferente. Lontano, un fischio di treno in manovra, forse alla stazione di Alpignano; un rombo di autocarro dalla parte di Pianezza, sulla strada di là dalla Dora.

Immobile in mezzo al viale, ascoltando questi rumori lontani e vicini, a poco a poco i suoi occhi si erano abituati all'oscurità. O forse, era la neve stessa che faceva luce. A parte alcune ombre nere e misteriose, sotto i gruppi piú folti dei sempreverdi, pini, cedri, magnolie, lecci, gli sembrava di vedere tutto come di giorno: soltanto senza colori.

Cominciò ad avanzare, adagio. Scorgeva, qua e là tra gli alberi, le aiole: grandi cerchi od ovali dove la neve aveva una forma convessa e pareva piú alta. Scorgeva, a intervalli regolari lungo il viale, da una parte e dall'altra, monticelli oblunghi dalle cui sommità affioravano le spalliere curve dei sedili di ferro. Poi una fontana gelata, un busto di pietra.

E scorgeva soprattutto, in fondo, verso destra, in un varco lasciato libero dai sempreverdi, attraverso le trame leggere e chiare degli alberi spogli, la grande facciata grigia della villa.

Ormai non era piú tanto lontana. Ancora cento passi, e ci sarebbe arrivato. Sarebbe arrivato, tra le aiole, le siepi e gli alberi, in quello slargo davanti alla villa, in quel parterre ai cui margini, sotto la grande magnolia, gli pareva di avere stretto tra le braccia l'infinito: Lina!

Osservando la facciata della villa, e incominciando a intravvedere le sagome delle finestre, il portichetto rococò, i balconi di ferro, improvvisamente si fermò spaventato, a un pensiero abbastanza naturale ma che

When he reached an avenue in the park, he stopped, his heart pounding, and once more listened to the silence: but now for a long, long time, as if in depth.

The air was still, clear and chilly. Nearby, the only sounds were the occasional cracking of boughs as they broke beneath the weight of fresh snow and the muffled thuds that followed: and, Lord knows why, the thuds and cracks had a kind of live, tortured quality. Far away the whistle of a train, shunting maybe in the station at Alpignano: the rumble of a lorry over towards Pianezza, on the road the other side of the Dora.

As he stood motionless in the middle of the avenue, listening to all these sounds, far and near, his eyes gradually became accustomed to the gloom. Or maybe it was the snow itself shedding light. Apart from some black, mysterious shadows under the thickest clumps of evergreens – pines, cedars, magnolias, holm-oaks – everything seemed to him as bright as day: but without the colours.

He began to move forward, slowly. Here and there among the trees he could make out flower-beds: great circles and ovals where the snow was convex in shape and appeared to be deeper. He noticed at regular intervals along both sides of the avenue oblong mounds from the top of which emerged the curved backs of iron park-benches. Then a frozen fountain, a stone bust.

And above all he noticed away to the right through the delicate clear tracery of naked trees, in a space left by the evergreens, the great grey front of the villa.

He was not so far away now. Another hundred metres and he would be there. There, among the flowerbeds, the hedges and the trees, in that open space in front of the villa, in that parterre at whose edge, beneath the great magnolia, he thought he embraced the infinite: Lina!

As he gazed at the façade of the villa and began to make out the outlines of the windows, the little rococo portico, the iron balconies, he suddenly stopped, terrified by a natural enough thought but which until then – maybe

fino a quell'attimo, forse per l'incanto dei ricordi o per la suggestione dell'ora e del luogo, non aveva attraversato la sua mente: e se nella villa c'era qualcuno?

Sapeva che durante la guerra, e per molto tempo dopo la guerra, era stata abitata, o meglio occupata, da alcune famiglie di sfollati, per tutto l'anno, anche durante l'inverno. Scaldavano con stufe le grandi sale, facevano la cucina nei caminetti: insomma, si erano adattati.

E se ce n'era rimasta anche soltanto una, di quelle famiglie?

O se c'era un custode, un giardiniere?

In questo caso, però, ci sarebbe stato, molto probabilmente, un cane. E il cane, ormai, dopo più di cinque minuti che aveva scavalcato il muro e che avanzava nel parco, avrebbe abbaiato, o almeno ringhiato dietro una porta, se lo tenevano chiuso. Invece, per quanto tendesse l'orecchio, non udiva niente.

Si ricordò, è vero, di aver sentito parlare di certi cani da guardia particolarmente intelligenti e feroci, che, senza muoversi, lasciano entrare il ladro o il forestiero nel recinto affidato alla loro custodia: lo lasciano avanzare quasi fino alla casa: lí, poi, a tradimento, gli balzano ai polpacci oppure alla gola.

Paura? Aveva paura? Con naturale trapasso di pensiero, si ricordò di sua moglie. Che cosa poteva temere, di più feroce? E sorridendo di sé, riprese a camminare.

Arrivò davanti alla villa. Avanzò di una decina di passi fino al centro del grande spiazzo vuoto. Qui, il chiarore della neve era anche più forte. Alzò gli occhi al cielo, come per cercarvi la luna e le stelle. Ma era nuvolo: unito, alto, grigio: e con un che di bianco, certo il riflesso della neve.

Dov'era la grande magnolia?

Era lí. Era lí a sinistra. Enorme, compatta, tutta intarsiata di bianco e di nero. I suoi rami più bassi, ca-

because of the magic of memories or the spell of time and place – had not crossed his mind: what if there was someone at the villa?

He knew that during the war and for a long time after the war it had been lived in or at any rate occupied by a number of evacuee families all the year round, winter included. They heated the great rooms with stoves, cooked in the fireplaces: in short, they made the best of it.

Now suppose just one of those families was still there?

Or what if there was a caretaker, a gardener?

In that case, though, there would very probably be a dog. And by now, after more than five minutes since he had climbed over the wall and walked through the park, the dog would have barked or at least growled behind a door if they had it shut in. But, though he strained his ears, he could hear nothing.

True, he remembered hearing about some particularly intelligent and ferocious watch-dogs which, without stirring, allow the thief or intruder to enter the grounds they guard: they let him almost reach the house: then they take him by surprise and leap at his legs or throat.

Afraid? Was he afraid? By natural association of ideas he remembered his wife. What was there fiercer to fear? And smiling at himself, he walked on.

He reached the villa. Ten metres farther and he stood in the centre of the wide empty space in front of the house. Here the brightness of the snow was still more intense. He looked up at the sky as if looking for the moon and the stars. But it was overcast – uniform, high, grey cloud: but with a touch of white, surely a reflection from the snow.

Where was the big magnolia tree?

It was there. There on the left. Enormous, solid, veneered in white and black. Its lowest branches, snow-laden, bent

richi di neve, arrivavano quasi a un metro dal suolo: sotto, si indovinava come una caverna vasta, profonda e completamente buia. Era lí, in quella caverna, che aveva sfiorato, per la prima e per l'ultima volta della vita, la vera felicità.

Guardando la caverna, a un tratto, quasi trasalendo, gli parve di ricordarsi di una certa frase che Lina gli aveva detto: e lui, a quella frase, aveva provato un bisogno improvviso di piangere di gridare di spaccare tutto: di fuggire con Lina in America, o in Australia, lui e lei soli, sposati, e ricominciare la vita laggiú, staccati da tutto quello che era stata la loro realtà fino allora. L'effetto era stato cosí forte che, subito dopo, aveva avuto paura. Aveva cercato di dimenticarsela, quella frase: presto, dopo qualche settimana, aveva cercato di dimenticare anche Lina. E c'era riuscito: ma soltanto per trent'anni.

Ecco, ora Lina era presente. Era viva, lí, con lui. E la frase ... la frase?

Chiuse gli occhi come per ricordarsela meglio: per ricordarsela esattamente, in ogni parola. Chiuse gli occhi, se li strinse in una mano, e fece un mezzo giro su se stesso, volgendo le spalle alla magnolia: anche questo per pensare meglio, per sfuggire alla tentazione di guardare la magnolia finché non si fosse ricordato la frase esatta: la magnolia, che lo affascinava, bianca, nera, greve, misteriosa, e che lo avrebbe distratto.

Dunque, Lina, a un certo momento, sciogliendosi dall'abbraccio, lo aveva fissato con i suoi occhi celesti e ridenti, lo aveva chiamato per nome e gli aveva sussurrato, quasi soffiato sul viso:

«Cosa direbbe tua mamma se ti vedesse qui?»

Ecco, ne era sicuro: non aveva avuto niente di piú bello, in tutta la vita.

Udí il rumore leggero di un passo sulla neve: il passo continuava, si avvicinava alle sue spalle. Provò un brivido: di terrore, e quasi di piacere, insieme. Sentí che doveva voltarsi: ma non ne aveva il coraggio. Forse,

down to within a metre of the ground: beneath you could glimpse a sort of vast, deep, pitch-dark cavern. It was there in that cavern that he had brushed true happiness for the first and last time in his life.

As he looked at the cavern, all at once with a start he seemed to remember a certain sentence that Lina had said to him: and on hearing it he had felt a sudden urge to weep, shout, go berserk: to run away with Lina to America or Australia, just the two of them, married and ready to make a fresh start, far from all that had been their reality till then. The effect had been so strong that immediately afterwards he had felt afraid. He had tried to forget that sentence: soon, after a few weeks, he had tried to forget Lina, too. And he had succeeded: but only for thirty years.

Now Lina was there. Alive, there, with him. And the sentence? . . . the sentence?

He closed his eyes in an attempt to remember, to remember it exactly, word for word. He closed his eyes, clasped his hand over them and half-turned with his back to the magnolia: this, too, was to help him think, to avoid the temptation of looking at the magnolia until he remembered the exact expression: for the magnolia which fascinated him, white, black, oppressive, mysterious, would distract him.

Well, Lina, at a certain moment slipping from his embrace, had looked straight at him with her laughing blue eyes, spoken his name and softly whispered, almost breathed on his face:

'What would your mother say if she saw you here?'

That was it, he was sure: in his whole life he could remember nothing more beautiful.

He heard the sound of a light footstep in the snow: then more steps that came up behind him. He shivered: it was terror yet at the same time something akin to pleasure. He felt that he must turn around, but he didn't

voltandosi, avrebbe visto. Oh, valeva la pena, non c'era dubbio. Ma il terrore era piú forte.

Il passo, ecco, si fermò vicinissimo, forse a meno di un metro dietro di lui. Gli parve di sentire come un soffio gelido nella nuca. Il vento?

Sentí che gli occhi, improvvisamente, gli si empivano di lacrime. Pietà! perdono! avrebbe voluto gridare. Non pietà e perdono perché credesse, anche in quel supremo momento, di aver fatto del male a Lina, lasciandola: ma pietà e perdono cosí, senza ragione, soltanto perché aveva paura. E Lina? Dov'era Lina adesso? Non aveva mai saputo piú niente di lei, ecco tutto: e non era una ragione per pensare che ...

Un fruscío, uno scalpiccío rapido, lievissimo, poi uno scricchiolío, uno schianto, un tonfo. Come se la persona che si era avvicinata a lui sulla neve, e che si era fermata alle sue spalle quasi da toccarlo, di colpo si fosse voltata e fosse fuggita via. O forse era la sua immaginazione: di vero c'erano soltanto lo schianto e il tonfo finale: un altro ramo, come tanti, che si era spezzato sotto il peso della neve. Forse un ramo della magnolia, questa volta: era proprio in quella direzione che sembrava fosse venuto il rumore.

Si volse, per controllare.

Si volse: e vide sulla neve, in linea diritta, davanti a sé, tra sé e la magnolia, le impronte nitide e fresche di due piedi piccoli, femminili: di passi che partendo dalla magnolia erano arrivati fino a lui, e poi erano tornati verso la magnolia.

Il primo istinto, si capisce, fu quello di correre alla magnolia. Ma non poté. Sentí che le gambe non lo avrebbero retto.

Il secondo istinto, di gridare.

Intanto, un fiocco, un altro: in un momento era ricominciato a nevicare.

Appena se ne sentí la forza, gridò:

«Chi è? Chi c'è lí?»

have the courage. Maybe, by turning around he would see. Oh, it was worth the effort, no doubt. But fear was stronger.

Now the steps stopped terribly near, perhaps less than a metre behind him. He seemed to feel an icy-cold breath on the nape of his neck. The wind?

He felt his eyes suddenly filling with tears. Have pity! Forgive me! – he wanted to cry out. Not pity or forgiveness because he believed even at that crucial moment that he had wronged Lina by leaving her: but pity and forgiveness for no particular reason, simply because he was afraid. And Lina? Where was Lina now? He had never heard of her since, that was that: and there was no reason to think that...

A rustling, a quick, gossamer light tread, then a creaking, a crack, a thud. As if the person who had approached him in the snow and stopped behind him, almost near enough to touch him, had abruptly turned and run away. Or maybe it was merely his imagination: the only real sounds were the crack and the final thud: another branch, like so many breaking beneath the weight of the snow. Perhaps a magnolia branch, this time: that was just the direction from which the sound had come.

He turned to see.

He turned and saw in the snow, in a direct line between him and the magnolia the fresh, clear prints of two small feet, a woman's: footprints that came up to him from the magnolia and then went back to the tree.

His first impulse, of course, was to run to the magnolia. But he couldn't. He felt that his legs wouldn't support him.

The second impulse was to shout.

Meanwhile, a snowflake fell, then another: a moment and it had started to snow again.

As soon as he felt strong enough, he called:

'Who is it? Who's there?'

Ma la sua voce si spense senza eco nell'aria feltrata dalla neve che ormai cadeva fitta.

Perché non aveva il coraggio di seguire le impronte dei piccoli passi fino alla magnolia?

Fra pochi minuti la neve le avrebbe cancellate, e lui non avrebbe mai piú saputo: avrebbe perso, con la prova che non era un'allucinazione e che quelle impronte erano vere, l'ultima occasione di sapere.

Ma forse era proprio questo il suo scopo. Non voleva sapere. Aveva paura di sapere.

Di corsa, affondando nella neve, incespicando, cadendo, continuando comunque, riattraversò il parco deserto, fino al muro, fino alla breccia: la scavalcò, e non si fermò finché non arrivò sulla piazza del paese, e non vide laggiú il verde del suo taxi, piccolo, lontano, nella luce d'oro del caffè davanti a cui lo aveva lasciato.

But his voice died away, echoless, in the air blanketed by the snow which was now falling heavily.

Why did he lack the courage to follow those little footprints up to the magnolia?

In a few minutes the snow would obliterate them and he would never know: he would lose, together with the proof that it was not a hallucination and that the footprints were real, the last opportunity of knowing.

But perhaps that was exactly his intention. He didn't want to know. He was afraid of knowing.

At a run, sinking deep in the snow, stumbling, falling, plunging on somehow, he crossed the deserted park to the gap in the wall: he clambered over and did not stop until he reached the village square and saw the small, distant, green shape of his taxi bathed in golden light, outside the café where he had left it.

NOTES ON ITALIAN TEXTS

THE REMOVAL (*Pratolini*)

1. This story, like Pratolini's most famous novel *Cronache di poveri amanti*, is concerned with the teeming life of the working classes in Florence. The city is an easily identifiable background: via de' Magazzini lies a stone's throw from the Piazza della Signoria on the northern side, and via del Corno immediately behind the Palazzo Vecchio on the eastern side.

2. In order to render a readable English version, it has occasionally proved necessary to make minor changes in punctuation or, as here, to insert a conjunction.

3. *Buonuscita*: generally signifies 'key money'; here, more specifically, a payment for surrendering a lease.

4. *Condominio*: lit., co-ownership (of a building composed of separate freehold flats etc.).

5. Palazzo Vecchio (or Palazzo della Signoria) – the fourteenth-century palace on the Piazza della Signoria which stands next to the Uffizi and is one of the landmarks of Florence.

6. *Mi accompagnai*: lit., I was keeping myself company. The notion of an action or a thing being companionable (a notion particularly applicable to children) can be expressed in the Italian language, but there is no equivalent English usage.

7. lit., opening.

8. lit., If you'll allow me.

9. Via de' Gondi, runs into the Piazza della Signoria, between the Palazzo Gondi and the Palazzo Vecchio.

10. The Italian *ottomana*, unlike the English ottoman, can generally also serve as a bed, and is therefore a large piece of furniture.

11. *Già*: a very common ejaculation in Italian, denoting agreement with varying degrees of emphasis.

12. lit., right up against.

13. In a household such as this, there would have been no heavy curtains as we know them. Instead there would be just coarse net curtains, which could be either caught back in loops, to let in more light, or allowed to hang down ('drawn') across the windows.

14. The Badia (church of a Benedictine abbey dating back to the thirteenth century) stands on the via del Proconsolo (parallel to via de' Magazzini), which leads into the Piazza Sanfirenze, at the back of Palazzo Gondi.

15. via dei Leoni, runs alongside the back of the Palazzo Vecchio.

16. lit., grazes.

17. *Vinsanto*: this is a local Tuscan word for any sweet wine – generally an inferior one, the kind of wine that has probably been kept for years and that old ladies might drink with a biscuit mid-morning.

HOUSES (*Cesare Pavese*)

Pavese's language, though deceptively simple, is rather difficult owing to its idiomatic character. His grammar and syntax are not always to be relied on, and he tends to use phrases familiar to him from his Piedmontese home.

1. *Se avessi lavorato* ...: as the sequel shows the tense is misleading.

2. *Tendendo l'orecchio*: a phrase which occurs twice and has no equivalent in English, indicating as it does a watchfulness for sound rather than a reaction such as 'pricking up one's ears' would imply.

3. *Andasse a sangue*: Tuscan idiom equivalent, though stronger, to *andare a genio*, which is in more general use, and indicating understanding as well as agreement.

4. *Ne era sperso*: a rather unusual expression which even Italians find it difficult to understand. Although *sperso* means 'lost' it here indicates a hankering back to the place.

5. *Girarne di case*: an idiomatic turn of phrase that conveys the idea of making the rounds of houses.

6. *Schioccò la lingua*: describes a typical Italian sound made to express appreciation of a drink.

7. *Prendere in giro*: generally conveys 'to make fun of', 'to pull someone's leg', but has a more specialized meaning in this context.

NOTES ON ITALIAN TEXTS
THE POOR (*Cassola*)

1. *Mura* (pl.): city-walls. cf. *muro* (masc. sing.), a wall (of a house).
2. *Discretamente*. cf. the French *discrètement*, it has something of Fowler's 'genteelism'. (See his *The King's English*, O.U.P.)
3. *Nobildonna*: the daughter of a nobleman, equivalent to 'Honourable'.
4. *Magari*: an elusive adverb with many idiomatic uses, for which see Shrewing's excellent *Italian Prose Usage* (C.U.P.) Here, and two lines later, it can almost be omitted in translation; it has a light emphasis, no more.
5. *L'Osservatore Romano*: newspaper; the official mouthpiece of the Vatican.
6. *Fascio*: the local headquarters of the Fascist party.
7. *Mica*: cf. the French *point*, emphasizing a negative.
8. 125 lire was a very small sum in Fascist times, less than the simplest English workman earned.
9. The Italian almost always employs the past conditional in an indirect statement, where we would use the conditional.
10. *Scapular*: long bands worn round neck by religious and semi-religious orders.
11. *Tertiaries*: lay Franciscan order, male and female.

BIG FISH, LITTLE FISH (*Calvino*)

1. *Dava puntì a tutti*: lit., gave everyone points.
1a. *Ci si poteva fidare a dargli roba in prestito*: lit., one could rely upon lending him things. *Roba* = things, stuff, also clothes, wares, property, money.
2. *Arnese*: lit., tool.
3. *Quel mar di scoglio*: lit., that sea of rock.
4. *E luccichii di branchi di rincorri-gli-ami*: lit., and twinkles of shoals of *rincorri-gli-ami*. *Rincorri-gli-ami*: lit., chase-the-hooks; Ligurian fishermen's dialect, used for very small fish in general.
5. *Mezz'acqua*: lit., between surface and sea-bed, i.e. not very deep.
6. *Tana*: lit., den, lair.
7. *Squadra*: also team, i.e. *squadra calcistica* = football team.
8. *Figurati*: also means, according to the context, 'Not at all', 'Just imagine!'.

9. *In gamba*: slang: also means, according to the context, bright, careful, clever, on one's toes.
10. *Struggimenti*: lit., longings.
11. *Zerli*: Ligurian fishermen's dialect. Very small fish of whitebait variety.
12. *Rocche*: Ligurian fishermen's dialect for rock-fish.
13. *Lazzaretto*: lit., lepers' hospital.

THE ASH OF BATTLES PAST (*Gadda*)

There is a profoundly classical background to Gadda's prose. So much is always made of his use of popular and dialect form that this element in his style is often overlooked. But it is particularly evident in this story. For instance, even the names – Eucarpio, Prosdocimo, Eulalia, have their Greek humorous meanings: Eucarpio as one who has done well for himself, Prosdocimo from whom much was expected, Eulalia the sweetly-spoken. The more one sees of Gadda's prose, the more one sees the many shades of meaning that he conveys in a single word.

1. *Commendatore*: recipient of an order of chivalry (*Ordine al merito della Repubblica Italiana*). Roughly equivalent to our O.B.E., but is largely awarded to prominent businessmen, and is regarded with some contempt. Often used for any stupid, pompous man.
2. *Urofinnici*: The Ugro-Finnic peoples are the westernmost branch of the Ural-Altaic races, and include Finns, Hungarians and the inhabitants of some Russian provinces. They were more or less excluded, by the racial theorists who inspired the German Nazis and Italian Fascists, from the condemnation attaching to most non-Aryan races, in particular the Semitic.
3. Monza: an industrial town near Milan, famous for the manufacture of cheap carpets.
4. *Lirette*: idiomatic diminutive of *lira*, used in a deprecating sense: 'Some few thousands', a sum easily afforded.
5. *Abiatici*: an archaic word, indicating descendants. *Abiatico*, strictly-speaking, refers to a son of a son of a daughter.
6. *Befana*: The *befana* is the little old woman believed by Italian children to bring them their presents on Twelfth Night. Although always depicted as ugly and in rags, she is not a witch, but a good fairy. In common usage the word is applied to any ugly woman. A corruption of *Epifania*, it is often used in popular speech for the Epiphany.

7. *Grana*: used idiomatically to indicate bother, trouble: the inference probably is that Eucarpio's old school-friends sometimes wanted to borrow money from him.

8. *Bellezza*: bellezza, bello, should not automatically be equated with 'beautiful', which is applied more strictly in English. *Una bella casa*, for instance, is a good, comfortable house, but is unlikely to have pretensions to actual beauty. The use in Italian is often subtle: *una bella donna* is a good-looking, perhaps a fine-looking woman; *una donna bella* may be really beautiful (but is more likely to be described as *bellissima*). In the present instance *la Bellezza di quegli anni* has the meaning rather of 'how good those times were' or 'what a grand time it was'.

9. *Poeta*: the reference is to D'Annunzio.

10. *Parenti serpenti*: literally, relations are serpents: not to be trusted. *Amici nemici* has much the same meaning (literally, friends are enemies).

11. Lit., 'would have cut his heart into just so many pieces for his school-friends; one for each of them'.

12. *Campanalismo*: A reference to love of one's bell-tower: in other words, of one's native town. The term is used to denote a parochial patriotism with deep social and political roots in Italy; born of the gatherings in a city's *piazza*, round the bell-tower, the sentiment is extended to embrace bitter inter-town or provincial rivalries of every sort, especially, nowadays, those of the football teams.

13. *Antiorbaciano*: orbace was the coarse woollen cloth, of Sardinian origin, from which the Fascists' uniforms were made. As such, it came to typify Fascism in common speech.

14. *Quel Tale*: 'That Man' or, 'That So-and-So': it is not easy to convey in English the underlying contempt and dislike. The reference is, of course, to Mussolini, to whom it was not always safe to refer by name.

15. *Mezzo migliaio*: lit., half a thousand.

16. *Parce sepulto, sepultae*: (Latin) 'Spare him, or her, in the grave', in other words, speak no ill of the dead. In this very latinized passage (in primis, deinde, etc.) *defunti* is used in a classical, and subtly different sense, from that of *morti*. The latter word refers, in a general way, to the dead; *i defunti* (from the Latin *de-fungi*) refers rather to those who, more recently, have come to the end of life and activity ('function' too is a derivative) but who are all very present in Eucarpio's mind.

17.   ... *declinato rose*: in Italian text-books of elementary Latin *rosa* is generally declined where the English primers choose *mensa*.

18.   *Ricostruzione immancabile*: lit., 'unfailing reconstruction'. One of the typical, vague phrases inspired by Mussolini in promising a future never attained by Fascism.

19.   *Banca d'interesse nazionale*: (or, *banca di diritto pubblico*): a para-statal corporation the profits of which do not go into private hands but are put into public works, etc.

20.   *Biscornuto*: not an Italian word, but taken over by the author from the French *biscornu*, meaning, etymologically, two-horned, but usually, when applied to animals, oddly or irregularly horned; hence its frequent use in the sense of *bizarre*. In the present case the simile of horns also conveys the suggestion of cuckoldry.

21.   Renzo and Lucia are the two principal characters of Manzoni's romance *I Promessi Sposi*.

22.   L'Adamello ... Isonzo: these are all well-known and hotly-contested battle-fields on the Italian front in the First World War.

23.   *Cecco Beppe*: familiar diminutives of the names Francesco and Giuseppe; a reference to the Emperor Franz Josef of Austria.

24.   *L'Adolfa*: this obviously refers to Adolph Hitler, but the feminine adjectival form is puzzling. It may be that *l'epoca*, or *l'età adolfa* is to be understood. Elsewhere, however, Gadda refers to *la belva adolfa* (the Adolphan wild beast) and it seems appropriate to use it in this sense here.

25.   *Orlando furioso*: Canto XXIII, verse I.

26.   U.P.I.M.: the Italian equivalent of Woolworth's. (*Unico Prezzo Italiano Milano*.)

27.   *I due*: refers to the two bravoes who threaten Don Abbondio in the first chapter of *I Promessi Sposi*. Manzoni devotes some pages to a description of the appearance and status of *bravi* in seventeenth-century Italy. They were usually hired cut-throats, or brigands in the pay of some local lord.

28.   *Stanare*: *tana* is a lair, den: *stanare* to dislodge from a den.

29.   *Gne ne disse*: dialect form of *gliene disse* (colloquial) – 'I told him off', 'spoke with extreme frankness to him', etc.

30.   *Nella neve*: lit., in the snow. The significance is, rather, 'you will die without a roof over your head'. Usually *sul lastrico*: on the pavement. Here there is deliberate over-emphasis to alarm the listener even more.

31. *Deluso*: *deludere* is more often used in the sense of 'to disappoint' than 'to delude'.
32. *Ho le ossa rotte*: lit., 'my bones are broken'. Always used in the sense of 'done for', 'worn out', etc.
33. *Cacatoio*: A vulgar word (shit-house).
34. Small pieces of natural coral, usually curved (hence the reference to *corno*, horn, which has its own sinister implication) are often worn in Italy as a protection against the Evil Eye. The significance of this scene in the story is that Prosdocimo, a nervous wreck after his war experiences, turns – half in earnest, half mockingly – to his coral charm to protect him from Eucarpio's wrath: which naturally infuriates Eucarpio, who would never have dreamed that he might be thought to have an evil effect on other people; indeed quite the reverse.
35. *Quel fregnetto*: Small object, bauble. (Roman dialect word.)
36. *Vox clamantis* (*in deserto*): Biblical quotation in Latin referring to St John the Baptist: 'A voice crying in the wilderness.' Prosdocimo ironically caps it with the one about casting pearls before swine: *ante porcos*.
37. *Dugentocinquantasei*: an archaic form, still used in Florentine dialect, of *duecentocinquantasei*.
38. Jean-Jacques Rousseau.
39. *Porca*: literally, the female of 'swine'. When applied to a woman, it indicates unchastity, harlotry.

THE MOTHER (*Ginzburg*)

1. *Liceo*: equivalent to French *lycée*, i.e. attended by pupils during the 3–5 years before entering a university.
2. *Si volevano molto bene*: *Volere bene a qualcuno*, to be very fond of, to love somebody (lit. to wish somebody well). A synonym, the phrase is ambiguous; it can be used when speaking of relatives and friends, also of somebody with whom one is in love, though without sexual implication.
3. *Ricreatorio*: youth club, recreation centre, for boys of all ages, usually run by priests.
4. *Saturnino Farandola, Robinson delle praterie*: titles of children's books belonging to a previous generation.
5. *Tutto quello che ci voleva*: lit., everything that one wanted (needed).

6. *Perché prima non erano capaci*: lit., because before they were not capable.

ANGUISH (*Moravia*)

1. *Manco morto. Manco* as noun; fault, defect. As adverb; less, not even. As adjective; lacking, and – in a different sense – left-handed (thus *manca*; left hand, left side).
2. *Avvocato*, lawyer; member of the legal profession, having right of pleading in courts, as barrister or solicitor.
3. *Se vuoi bene a tuo fratello*. See note 2 under The Mother.

FOOTSTEPS IN THE SNOW (*Soldati*)

1. *È una goccia che fa traboccare il vaso*: lit., 'it's a drop that makes the jar overflow'.
2. *Guarino Guarini*: born in 1624 at Modena, lived mostly at Turin and died in Milan in 1683. A Baroque architect, also a professor of philosophy and mathematics. Designed the Palazzo Carignano in Turin as well as churches in Paris and Lisbon.
3. *Vincenzo Gioberti*: philosopher and politician. Born in Turin in 1801. Died in Paris in 1852. He was exiled for his liberal views. His chief aims were to arouse the forces of liberalism, free Italy from foreign domination and form a federal union of the Italian states. His book *The Civil and Moral Primacy of the Italians* (1843) came to be regarded as 'the bible' of Mazzini and the revolutionaries.
4. *Filippo De Pisis*: Born in Ferrara in 1896. Died in Milan in 1956. Italian painter with a literary background. Associated as a writer with Chirico, Carrà and others of the metaphysical school movement in Ferrara. Much of his work belongs to the Impressionist and Post-Impressionist traditions.
5. *C'era di mezzo la villeggiatura*: lit., holidays were involved.
6. *. . . Senza proporsi una meta*: lit., without aiming at a goal.
7. *Cammina e cammina*: this expression remains invariable for all persons, singular and plural.
8. *Quell'angolo, appunto, etc*: lit., that corner, to be exact, where the arcades of the two main streets reached, meeting but not proceeding further, after fourteen kilometres employed

to cross the city and to climb from the banks of the Po the gentle slope upon which it is built.

9. *Rebrousser chemin*: retrace one's steps, turn back.

10. *La belva*: lit., the wild beast.

11. *Case a riscatto*: 'redeemable' houses. Houses that can become the property of owner-tenants in the same way that mortgaged houses in Great Britain can.

12. *Falansteri*: French, *phalanstères* – communal dwellings which formed part of an ideal cooperative life preached by the French philosopher and socialist writer Charles Fourier (1772–1837). In Italian the word has a pejorative connotation.